Bread is Not Enough

by

KITTY PRIDE

HODDER AND STOUGHTON
LONDON SYDNEY AUCKLAND TORONTO

 Printed in Great Britain for Hodder and Stoughton Limited, St. Paul's House, Warwick Lane, London EC4P 4AH by Cox & Wyman Ltd, London, Reading and Fakenham.*

Preface

HUNGER IS AN acute problem. Throughout the world there are many minority peoples who live where food supplies are inadequate and medical help is limited. But while these people have great physical needs, the Christian knows that they also have deep spiritual needs. Anyone who has experienced for himself the spiritual life and guidance to be found in the Christian Scriptures, longs to share this with others. He believes that the Scriptures are the answer to the spiritual hunger of every man, whatever his language. In going to live with such a minority group, his purpose is to give them something more than bread and medicine — the chance to know God for themselves, and to talk to Him in their own language.

This book is about one such group — the Chatino Indians of southern Mexico — and what it has meant to take them . . . more than bread.

Wycliffe's first attempt to begin work among the Chatinos took place in 1942. A new worker, accompanied by a senior translator, set out to survey the area. The prospects seemed promising, the new worker was well-received and invited to return with his wife and baby to learn the language. On the journey back to Mexico City this man became ill and in forty-eight hours he had died.

The following year another couple was assigned to the

Chatinos. They settled in a nearby trading centre and from there made frequent trips 1000 feet up the mountainside to the nearest Chatino settlement. However after two years they were invalided home.

In 1946 a third team took over the work. Armed with his predecessor's language notes, Howard McKaughan was soon accepted by the Chatinos as a friend. Two years later the family was invited to live in the Chatino town of Yaitepec, where they shared the home of a Chatino family. Howard visited many towns and villages and became known throughout the mountain area. He worked on the analysis of the language and produced an alphabet and a small Chatino–Spanish dictionary. Five years went by and Howard was asked to lead Wycliffe's new advance in the Philippines. And so another couple was assigned to continue his work.

Thus in 1952 Bill and Jay Upson were introduced to the Chatinos by Howard, who was able to see them safely installed in a home of their own. Bill and Jay inherited all Howard's language materials, the goodwill of the people and a thriving medical practice. The Upsons continued language learning and analysis. Then in 1959 Leslie and Kitty Pride joined the Chatino team to investigate rumours that there were 'other Chatinos' who spoke another dialect and who might require a separate translation.

As you read this book and are introduced to some of these lovable Chatino people (and the unlovable ones too) you will catch a glimpse of what it means to provide a minority group with . . . more than bread.

Contents

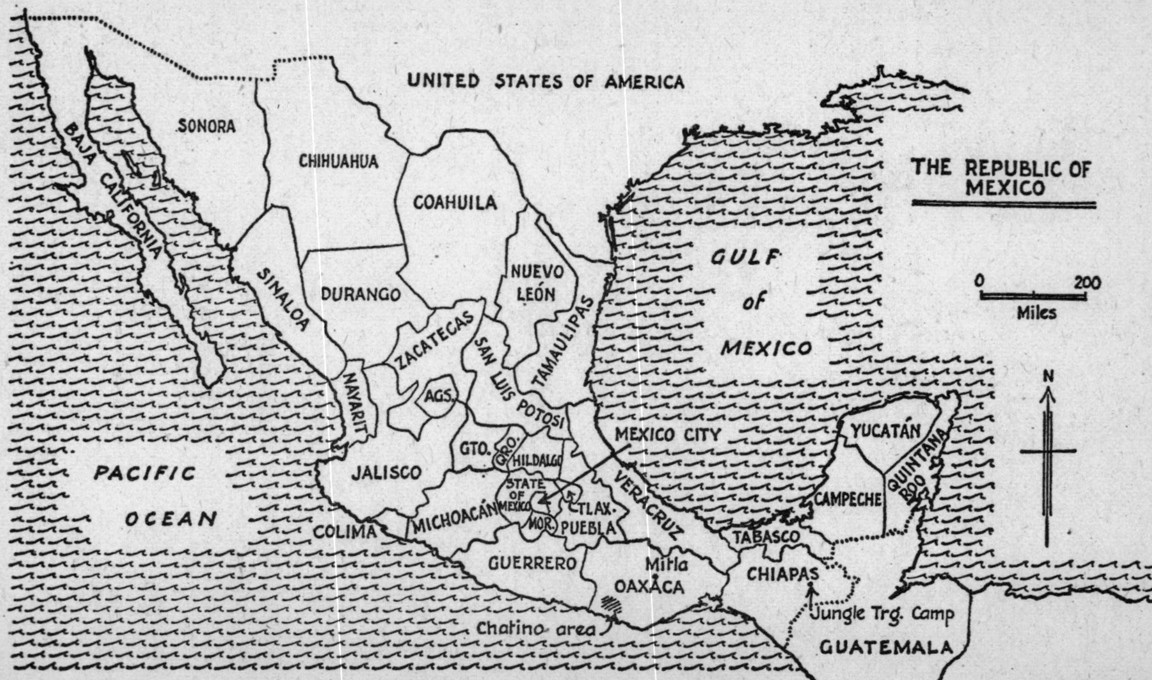
THE REPUBLIC OF MEXICO
UNITED STATES OF AMERICA
GULF of MEXICO
PACIFIC OCEAN
0
200
Miles
N
SONORA
BAJA CALIFORNIA
CHIHUAHUA
COAHUILA
NUEVO LEÓN
TAMAULIPAS
SINALOA
DURANGO
ZACATECAS
SAN LUIS POTOSI
AGS.
NAYARIT
JALISCO
GTO.
QRO.
HILDALGO
STATE OF MEXICO
MEXICO CITY
TLAX.
MOR.
PUEBLA
VERACRUZ
MICHOACÁN
COLIMA
GUERRERO
Mitla
OAXACA
Chatino area
TABASCO
CHIAPAS
Jungle Trg. Camp
GUATEMALA
CAMPECHE
YUCATÁN
QUINTANA ROO

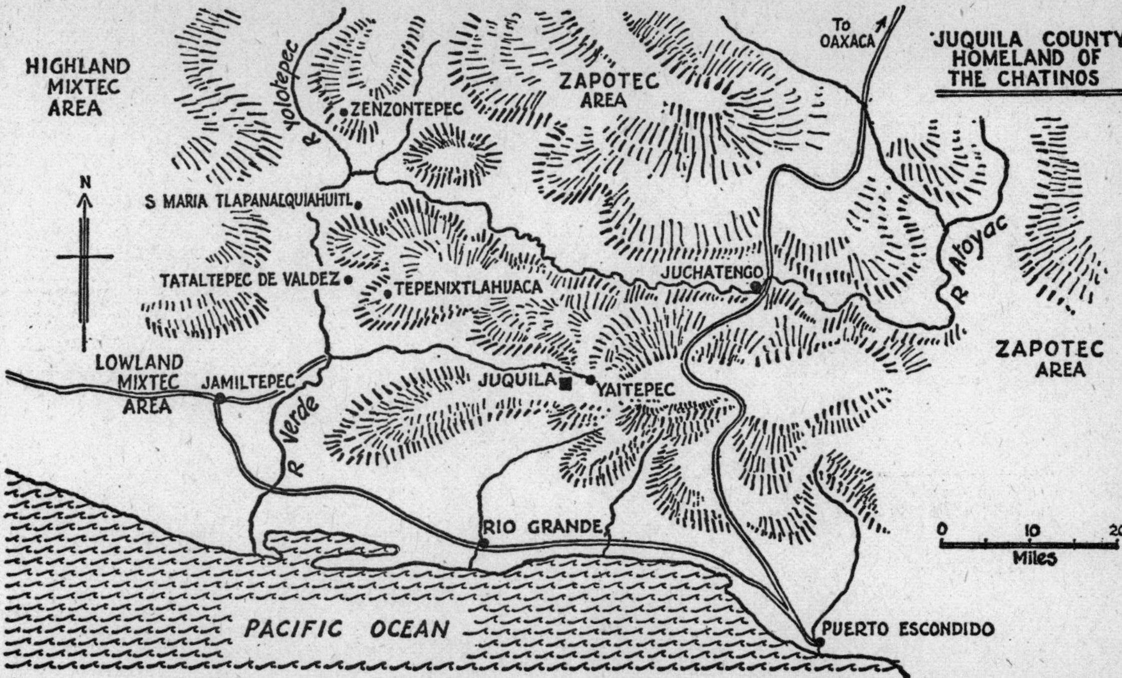

'JUQUILA COUNTY
HOMELAND OF
THE CHATINOS
HIGHLAND
MIXTEC
AREA
ZAPOTEC
AREA
ZAPOTEC
AREA
LOWLAND
MIXTEC
AREA
To
OAXACA
N
R Yolotepec
R Atoyac
R Verde
ZENZONTEPEC
S MARIA TLAPANALQUIAHUITL
TATALTEPEC DE VALDEZ
TEPENIXTLAHUACA
JUCHATENGO
JUQUILA
YAITEPEC
JAMILTEPEC
RIO GRANDE
PUERTO ESCONDIDO
PACIFIC OCEAN
0
10
20
Miles

PART ONE

Mexican Mountains

1

Why Mexico?

'Is your mother still alive, then?'

'Oh yes. Look, here is her photo on the wall.'

Pause, as the woman examined our picture gallery, snaps of relatives and friends, all in one big frame.

'And your home-town really is on the other side of the sea?'

'That's right.'

'But it's so very far away — why did you come?'

I told her for the umpteenth time.

'But what did your mother say? She must be very sad.'

'She is sad that she can't see me every day, but she wanted me to do what God wanted, because she is interested and concerned about you Chatino people too.'

'Oh. Does she know about me?'

'Yes, because I write to her every week, and she writes to us every week.'

'Do you mean that she can read and write too? Yes, well, that is a good thing. When you write, tell her that we are glad you are here to help us, because the children get ill so often and very quickly die when you aren't here — so we will look after you, tell her. I wouldn't want my daughter to go to the other side of the sea. I don't want her to go to any other town at all. Why, she might die there, and then her soul would never find its way back here to her home-town! Tell your mother that I don't think you will die here because you have so much medicine, but, if you did, you have your house here and belong to this town now, so we would bury you properly in the town cemetery and remember you at the All Souls fiesta, so she mustn't worry about all that.'

I thanked her for her thoughtfulness and concern for my mother and me. Then I told her that I would certainly see my mother again in heaven, anyway. I said that it didn't really matter where I died at all. I told her again that I belonged to Jesus Christ, and that Christians have something to look forward to. She listened, puzzled, and could not understand why I was not afraid.

Later that day, I thought about my conversation with this woman, Chona. Now, why had I come? My reasons had not made much impression on Chona. Were they valid? Did God really want me here in Tataltepec?

I thought back to a certain Covenanter Bible class in England. What a tremendous help those leaders had been in my teenage years. About a year after I became a Christian, a missionary speaker had challenged us, and a few weeks later I found the courage to tell our leader that I thought God wanted me to be a missionary. She was not discouraging, but neither was she wildly enthusiastic, and I was most disappointed. For years I had wanted to be a veterinary surgeon. I worked hard at school with that end in view, and that end only. Now I thought that she ought to be thrilled with all my potential as a veterinary surgeon; what a marvellous missionary I would make with so much to offer! This missionary idea was terrific, because I was quite sure that the world was desperately in need of missionary veterinary surgeons.

Some time later, I began to be aware of Mexico. I saw things about the country in the newspapers and in magazines, I heard about it on the wireless, and people mentioned it in conversation, but no one else seemed to be so constantly reminded of the place. The awful thought struck me—surely God does not want me to go to Mexico? No British people ever go *there*! Anyway, I was sure no mission worked there, and they certainly would not want a missionary vet . . .

I did not dare to share this dreadful suspicion with anyone, but mysteriously a magazine called *Translation* started appearing in our home. I opened it idly and found articles by missionary translators working in Mexico. I was quite annoyed at first, and felt that God was playing with me.

'All right,' I told Him, 'so there are missionaries in Mexico translating the Bible, but they are all Americans, and I am sure they are not interested in a vet!'

Surreptitiously I continued to read the magazine, but stubbornly I refused to ask where it came from or how it had arrived at our home. Much later I discovered that the former leader of the local Boy Covenanters' class, Phil Cheesman, had gone to Canada and joined the Wycliffe Bible Translators there. Now he was working with them in Peru. My brother corresponded with him as the class 'scribe', and so the magazines had arrived in our home.

Meanwhile, I was working hard in the sixth form at school and thoroughly enjoying my science subjects. However, my exam results were disappointing, certainly not veterinary college standard, so I went to work as a junior technician at a veterinary laboratory. I went to evening classes at the local Technical College to try to attain the required standard.

I was still fighting the idea of Mexico when a Mexican vet visited the laboratory. This was a shock, and then I was asked to demonstrate some particular technique to him. He watched carefully, made notes, and said: 'Have any of you technicians ever thought of coming to Mexico? We really want to set up a research centre like this, and we could do with some trained technicians.' I don't remember what I replied, but I was flabbergasted to think that, quite apart from any Christian ideas, Mexico seemed to be a place of employment to take into consideration.

One evening, I had arrived back at my digs, dead beat after cycling home from the Tech. My landlady greeted me with:

'Now, just sit down in that armchair and look at the telly. You need to relax, and I'll bring you a nice hot cup of Ovaltine. It's a programme from the World Health Organisation, so I know you will want to see it.'

I slumped down in the chair and took the hot drink. Then I glanced at the screen and almost leapt out of the chair again. I wanted to run and hide, but the Ovaltine in my hand, and my landlady's kindness, stopped me. There it was, 'W.H.O. in Mexico.' I watched the programme and went up to bed. I realised that I had to make a decision. Other people were not confronted by Mexico wherever they turned, day after day, year after year. It just could not be coincidence any longer. I told God that I would go to Mexico if He really wanted me there, but as a vet. This had been such a long battle, that it was a tremendous relief to give in, but when I told my boy-friend all about it, he was not impressed. 'Oh, I can wait, and you'll grow out of it,' he said.

The evening studies went well. The mock exams were not too bad, but the actual exam results were not encouraging. Gradually I realised I never would get to veterinary college. I felt that I should take a more positive attitude towards Mexico, and I started finding out about the Christians there, and about Christian work. I remembered the *Translation* magazines, and thought that at least W.B.T. could give me some information about Mexico, even if they were not interested in Britons becoming members. (I had quite forgotten Phil Cheesman still in Peru.) Late in 1952, I wrote to their office and, early in 1953, the answer came. Did I know that the Wycliffe Language Course was starting in London in July 1953? Dr. Kenneth Pike had worked in Mexico and would be there. He would be glad to give me an interview and answer all my questions.

Sitting in our house in Tataltepec all those years later, I remembered clearly the feeling of inevitability as I read that first letter from the Wycliffe office. Again the Lord had cut the ground of excuses away from under my feet — here was the Language Course to be held in Britain, so it wasn't just for Americans. (I soon discovered that Canadians, Australians and New Zealanders were already involved anyway . . .) I went to the Open Day of that first Wycliffe Language Course. There I had talked to George Cowan, who was part of the team translating the Scriptures for the Mazatec people in Mexico. I saw the film *Oh for a Thousand Tongues*, which showed something of Wycliffe translators in Mexico, and I suddenly realised that there were still more unwritten languages in Mexico, and that the people who spoke them knew nothing of God's Word. Then I knew that I should go there as a Bible translator and not as a veterinary surgeon.

Eagerly I plied Mr. Cowan with questions.

'Well, you need some Bible training first. Then you must do this linguistics course, and during that summer you can make formal application to W.B.T.; but keep in touch with us in the meantime.'

Two women were also at that Open Day who had been told by a mutual friend to look out for me. One was about to start the course at, and the other was an old student of, Redcliffe Missionary Training College. The latter was now doing the Language Course during her furlough from Africa, as she was about to embark on translation work too. Both urged me towards Redcliffe, but I had my own ideas. Although I promised to go and visit the one about to start training there, I was privately making my own list of requisites for the lucky college that would get me to train! It was to be a biggish Bible college, where one could work for nationally recognised qualifications — co-educational of course, not a boarding-school kind of place — and not to do with any particular denomination or organisation.

I went home to start finding out addresses of colleges. I would write to the lot for their prospectuses, and then decide which fitted my requirements best. Redcliffe? Nuts! As I remember this bit, I always smile to myself at how easily God had foiled my self-centred plans. How patient He is in the face of such arrogance as mine. It seems ridiculous now, but when I was planning my own training programme, I just could not find out any Bible college addresses other than Redcliffe. I remember thinking, 'Oh well, to be fair I really should add their prospectus to the pile, so I'll just write for it meanwhile.'

In a few days the prospectus arrived as requested, but accompanied by a letter from the principal. 'When I just write for information, why can't these people leave it at that?' — I thought with irritation, and then some lines from the letter jumped right out and hit me:

> There is only one college at which the Lord can train you. If He tells you to come to Redcliffe, we shall be glad to hear from you, but find out where He wants you to go. We shall be praying for you.

I was shocked to the core. When one needs training, one chooses the college with the appropriate courses, I had thought. Now, for the first time in my life, I asked God to choose for me. I spread that letter out, knelt down and really prayed. I had always known what I wanted to do, and made my own decisions, willing to take the consequences if things happened to turn out badly, and not quibbling to manipulate other people as necessary. I suddenly realised that this did not add up to wanting to do what God wanted me to do, and it was a nasty shock. I did go to Redcliffe, and it was certainly the right place for me. Once, in my second year, I was asked to give my testimony, particularly with reference to what God had taught me at college. Afterwards the Vice-Principal said to me, 'Did you never have any trouble getting along with fellow students, Kitty?'

'Only one, and she left at the end of my second term,' I replied, rather surprised and a bit smugly.

'A pity,' said the Vice-Principal, 'but did it never occur to you that perhaps other students had trouble getting on with you?'

I did not reply, but it never had occurred to me. It dawned

on me that my fellow students were not just college furniture, but were learning and training as much as I was. They had their joys and their black patches as much as I did. I really cared about the children in my Sunday school class, and about the women at the meeting where two of us helped each week. I prayed earnestly for all of these, chatted to them, and wanted to get to know them, but when did I ever pray for my fellow students? When I had first applied to Redcliffe, I had told my boy-friend about it, and discovered that he was still waiting for this Mexico-missionary phase of my life to wear off. It had all been rather dramatic, as by now we had almost drifted into an engagement, but my bombshell effectively broke that up. I had not advertised this at college, but now that I began to get to know the others as individuals, I found that what I had thought to be very noble of me was in fact quite commonplace, and others had coped with far more difficult situations.

In my last term at Redcliffe, I found that seniority brings responsibility. I had held various positions of minor leadership through the years, and it had never worried me, because I well knew how to manipulate people. Now I was faced with responsibility in God's Name, and I realised that just manipulating students as necessary would not help the college, or them, or me, or God, one iota. So I had to ask God's help and direction for something that I had thought that I knew how to do, and I found that He also gave me special wisdom and ability for what I knew that I ordinarily could not do. The Bible had become very precious to me, and more and more I looked forward to helping to translate it into the language of a people who had never had the Scriptures before.

College ended, so had my money, and there were only three months till the Wycliffe Language Course began. I went home to the farm and took a job with a neighbouring farmer, looking after his small dairy herd. I really enjoyed being back on the farm, coping with ringworm on the bullocks and warble fly on the cows' backs! When the first pay-day came, I was rather shattered to find that the farmer thought that he was just employing me as casual, part-time labour. If this continued, I would certainly not have enough money for the Language Course so I started looking round for another job. A friend of my father's needed a helping hand to tide him over on a chicken farm for a week or two, and then I met a forester and got a forestry job in the tree nursery. It was an unskilled job, but nothing else had turned up, and I thought, 'Well, God will have to do a miracle to provide those Language Course fees!' I could not quite understand why I was enjoying my work so much, and so at peace about it all, since I was obviously not going to earn enough money. At the end of the first week, the forester came rushing up to the nursery again, all smiles — he had already paid me, and I was puzzled.

'I've got a new job for you,' he said. 'Now, if I lend you these books this weekend, you must gen up on seed-beds and planting tree seeds, and then you will be an expert by Monday.'

'What *do* you mean?' I asked in amazement.

'Well, our estates' head office has just phoned to say that they have put a whole consignment of tree seeds on the train, and I have to pick them up this afternoon. They have to be planted immediately, as it is already pretty late in the year for sowing tree seeds.'

'So?' I asked, not getting the drift of his argument at all.

'So, I am the only expert here at the moment, and I don't have time to personally make seed-beds and plant seeds. I have two gangs of men out on contract, and my last two men are expert tree fellers, working alone. So you must become an expert too, and I'll put you in charge of the nursery and these seeds, and give you two men as your assistants. I'll come and give you regular advice, never fear — it's not hard to grow trees. Oh yes, and I'll have to promote you, of course, which means a fifty per cent increase in pay.'

Dumbfounded, I took the books, and I was delighted to

find that they had process photographs as illustrations, as well as plenty of diagrams. We planted the seeds according to book, and the sun beat down mercilessly day after day, so we built 'shade hedges' of birch branches, also according to book, and then it started to rain. Our seedlings came up, and most of them thrived. And so, God had provided my fees.

Once more I left home. The Language Course at last, and the opportunity to put in my application for the Wycliffe Bible Translators. What would I learn at the Course? A leaflet said:

> Linguistic training is provided by the Summer Institute of Linguistics through its Schools. The student is taught to recognise and reproduce speech sounds, including those not found in European languages, devise an alphabet and analyse complicated grammatical structures. Tuition is also given in the techniques of language learning, the construction of simple reading materials and in anthropology.

Mr. Cowan had said that those of us applying to join the Wycliffe Bible Translators would get information classes on Saturday mornings. We did, and learnt how God had first made Cameron Townsend, the colporteur, aware of people in Central America who could not use his books because they could not understand the national language, and thought that the God of the Bible could only speak Spanish, so they sadly refused to buy. Townsend realised that they spoke a language as yet unwritten, and that books were entirely foreign to them. He was determined to prove to them that God could speak their language too, and was really concerned about them. So he left his Bible-selling job, learnt the Cakchiquel language, wrote it down, and translated the New Testament into it. He became very conscious of the many other unwritten languages spoken in the world, and of the millions of forgotten people who spoke them. Some groups had only a handful of speakers, others had half-a-million speakers, but all were people that God wanted to speak to. Mr. Townsend found a kindred spirit in Mr. L. L. Legters from the U.S.A. They began to interest others in these neglected peoples, and set up the first Summer Institute of Linguistics to prepare future translators by teaching them a scientific method for learning unwritten languages. Work was started in Mexico in the 1930s, although the Wycliffe Bible Translators were not formed as an organisation until 1942. Mr. Cowan himself joined the first translators there in the 1940s, and now in the 1950s Wycliffe had branched out into several other countries, and had started this linguistics course in Britain.

In one place the application form said, 'Field of Preference', and then three lines labelled 1., 2., 3. So I wrote:

1. Mexico
2. Mexico
3. Mexico

It was strongly suggested that I put at least one alternative, but, after all those years of fighting God on this point, I had no alternative suggestion to offer. I thoroughly enjoyed the linguistics, although I was never in the top stream. It all seemed so reasoned and scientific, and I found that my laboratory training helped just by giving a scientific research approach.

Leslie Pride was also taking the course that summer of 1956. I had known him vaguely for several years, and we had many mutual friends and acquaintances. He was even a member of the church where I had attended the Covenanter class, but we had never really got to know each other before. One day I was jolted into an acute awareness of him because he asked me to marry him. I had decided that, after my previous experience of boy-friends, marriage was out for me, and now, right out of the blue, the issue was before me again when I least expected it. For his part Leslie had apparently been very aware of me from the first day of the course, and had been praying for some time for God's direction with regard to a wife. He too was in the process of application to

W.B.T. that summer, and as I got to know him better, and we prayed together, marriage did not seem quite such a crazy proposition after all. We agreed that, if only one of us was accepted, that was that, but I felt more and more ready to say 'Yes' to him, if we were both accepted. Leslie was obviously quite sure that I was the wife that God had chosen for him, and I was getting more and more persuaded.

The course ended in September, Leslie returned to University, and I did some supply teaching in South London. Not that I was a teacher, but the flu was so bad that autumn that they were desperate for people to fill in. Not until early December did we hear the results of our applications. Lots of phone calls were made that evening as we applicants tried to contact each other with the good news; and as Leslie and I got engaged in our phone call, that news was passed round too. Christmas was a time of meeting each other's families and getting to know each other better. Leslie had to finish that year at Cambridge University and then do a year's Bible College training, but I had completed my training, had no steady job and no other direction from God. A course at Wycliffe's Jungle Camp in Southern Mexico was the next step, and the last course for that winter began on February 20th in Mexico City. If I did some deputation to acquaint interested friends with what the Wycliffe Bible Translators was all about so that they could pray intelligently, and if I got together the passage money, equipment and three months' support, it seemed that it was time to go. We would wait and marry when Leslie joined me in Mexico. One other couple, Desmond and Grace Derbyshire, were expecting to go then, but it seemed pretty impossible that I would be ready. However, bookings were made for the three of us on the *Queen Elizabeth*, to sail on February 8th. Late in January, mine was cancelled, as the whole idea looked so improbable. But on February 1st, I received the last of the money, and I had acquired the necessary equipment, but I had no visas. Due to a misunderstanding at the Mexican Consulate, I was refused papers there, and the American

Consulate would not give a transit visa without evidence that I could and would leave that country. A cable to the director in Mexico — and the help of a government official there — caused another cable to be sent to the Mexican Consulate in London which cleared up the misunderstanding. It was now February 7th. A rush to the American Consulate, only to be told:

'I'm afraid papers for Mexico don't prove that you really will leave the U.S. in the specified time. I need more concrete evidence of your travel plans, to issue a visa.'

Rather desperate now, but sure that I should be leaving, I prayed as I walked along the street, and then phoned the Derbyshires, who were all set to leave for Mexico the following day. Des said:

'I know! Let's rush over to American Express and buy your bus ticket from New York to Mexico City. I've got the old Wycliffe van here, so I'll come and collect you.'

At American Express, we pooled our spare money and managed to buy the bus ticket. Then, back to the American Consulate just before it closed. The visas at last! We phoned the Wycliffe office, only to learn of the complete cancellation of my booking on the *Queen Elizabeth*. What now? Surely God had not arranged these visas at the last minute for nothing? 'Ask the office for the address of the shipping agent,' said Des. 'We'll go down there and see if they have a cancellation or something.' As we tried to drive through the rush hour in central London, the office phoned the shipping agents to warn them of our coming, and one fellow stayed behind to help us. We got there at 6.00 p.m. Somehow he had found a berth on a Dutch ship for the next day. It was impossible for me to get from my home to London the next morning in time to catch the boat train, so he arranged with the shipping line for me to arrive at Southampton docks at the last minute. Des took me back to Waterloo Station, and then rushed home to help his wife finish their packing. I phoned the news to Leslie and a few other key friends, then went home to tell my family and finish packing.

From the send-off in London the next morning one would have thought that it had been planned for months. Leslie was there, and a group came from Redcliffe. The Vice-Principal disappeared and, in a few minutes, was back with a return ticket to Southampton for Leslie. It was so thoughtful of her — we had had so little time together. At Southampton Central Station, we were met by the Docks' Missionary, mobilised by yet another kind friend, and he whisked us off to the docks. Earlier he had delivered flowers and cards to my cabin from yet more friends, and had told the officials that he was going to meet me from the train. Everyone else was on board, so they quickly hustled me through, and within half-an-hour I had left England.

The Derbyshires had arranged to meet me in New York, as the *Queen Elizabeth* was to dock a day earlier, but terrible Atlantic gales delayed all shipping, and there was a dockers' strike in New York, so the *Queen Elizabeth* was sent to Halifax instead, and I next saw the Derbyshires in Mexico City! The American immigration man was decidedly grumpy the day we arrived:

'Transit?' he said, when he saw my papers. 'Well, it should only take you five days to get out of the country.' And he stamped 5 DAYS on the visa. Kind relatives met me and took me to their home in Long Island for one delightful night — but no Derbyshires, travelling alone, only four days left to get to the Mexican border, and what then? God had managed arrangements so well up to now that I did not really doubt the outcome, but I thought that I had better get started. So my relatives saw me on to the Greyhound long-distance bus in New York. I had wondered what happened to bus travellers' luggage, but an American Express agent had met the boat too, and collected up the heavy luggage of all A.E. passengers — another provision before I had even known of the necessity. Now, for the first time, I saw how high these great buses were, and the great maw underneath, open to receive the cargo. My two trunks, two duffle bags and suitcase looked quite insignificant in there. I just stayed on that bus, getting off only when we had to change. So, by the time we had crossed Texas to the border town of Laredo, I was getting pretty used to American bus travel. In order to cross the border, we had to claim all our luggage and transfer to the Mexican bus waiting to take us across the international bridge. Two trunks, two duffle bags, and no suitcase. . . !

'You'll just have to wait, Ma'am, till the next bus comes in following the same route. They must have missed transferring it somewhere. It'll be here in six hours.'

It was with a sinking feeling that I saw the bus for Mexico City pull out without me, and realised that I had just one more day to 'get out of the country', as that immigration man had put it. The six hours passed, the suitcase arrived, and there was another bus for Mexico City standing outside. We crossed the bridge and the Mexican immigration officers were most polite and helpful. Not so the 'red-caps' (porters)! When they tried my small wooden chest filled with books, they determined on a fat tip. I was bewildered by the impassioned Spanish of the four gesticulating red-caps surrounding me, and then an attractive girl stepped forward and said:

'Are you having trouble? Perhaps I can help you.'

I explained, and her voluble Spanish soon had the red-caps organised and my luggage back inside the bus. She told me how much to tip them, and quelled their expostulations with a look. Estela was a Mexican, and it turned out that she and her sister and cousin were just returning home with her mother after a year of English study near Niagara Falls. As I was travelling alone, they graciously invited me to join their party and so avoid anyone else wishing to take advantage of my ignorance, like those red-caps.

'I like to obtain an English daughter,' said Mamá.

Soon we all piled into the bus and found our reserved seats. Mamá and the girls made it obvious to everyone, but without embarrassing me, that I belonged with them. Later I realised how extremely kind they had been to take on a total stranger like that. They were not the ones to point out with horror that a girl never travels alone in Mexico, particularly on public transport. They just remedied the situation.

As we moved out into the countryside, I realised that I was in Mexico at last. A great sense of joy and peace flooded over me, and I just sat there praising the Lord my God in my heart. I experienced a feeling of home-coming, with an eagerness to get to know the people of this vast, sunny land. I certainly did not feel alone or lonely, and I thanked God again and again for the tremendous privilege of being there. Estela and the others made that twenty-two-hour trip so easy for me that it was a delight.

'This is Monterrey. Come on, let's have something to eat. There's plenty of time, and we'll order for you.'

They did, and I remarked how delicious my first Mexican meal tasted. They went off into peals of laughter, and Estela explained:

'You will have to get used gradually to our Mexican hot chile peppers, so I ordered "American style" for you.' So much for my first Mexican meal!

At the Mexico City bus station they were met by Papá, but none of them would leave until I had phoned the Wycliffe H.Q., and they knew that someone was coming to collect me. These people have been our good friends ever since, and our mentors in matters of national custom. When they heard about my fiancé, they were delighted, and immediately made me promise to bring Leslie to see them as soon as he arrived in Mexico. I visited them several times before that day dawned, and they took a great interest in what we were doing. They confessed that most people in Mexico City knew very little about the people living in the remote villages of their own country. They just assume that such people all speak the national language, Spanish, and are conversant with the same things as a city-dweller. Most Mexicans are very proud of their Indian heritage, but tend to think of it as past history which gave a basis for present-day regional customs and costumes, but that the languages have died out.

Everything was new to me, and first impressions of Mexico were rather kaleidoscopic, but all the time I felt that I belonged. The welcome at the H.Q. underlined all this, and increased the feeling of being at home. I had really arrived at last.

2

Wedding, and Then?

THE TWO YEARS after my arrival in Mexico City had passed very quickly, with weekly letters to and from Leslie. We sometimes wondered just where and with whom we would be working after we were married, but we were both well occupied, and the distance between us was just too big to allow us to consider the matter very seriously until we were together again. Then, suddenly I was back in the City again, and his arrival was imminent. Everyone at the H.Q. wanted to know just when he would arrive, but I could only tell them the day the boat left England, when it was due to dock in New York, and then just calculate the time for the coach journey from there. All were agog to meet my fiancé, and one morning at coffee break a Canadian couple did a skit in their best Oxford accents of Leslie and Kitty meeting each other with hand-shaking and back-slapping in the jolly British fashion! I was amused by their antics, but privately appalled at the thought of what awful jokes they might think up next.

Sitting at lunch the next day, someone rushed into the dining room and said:

'Quick, phone for you, Kitty.'

I leapt up and began to run, then I slowed down abruptly, as I thought, 'It's too soon. He can't be here yet. It must be that fellow having me on again to see what I'll say on the phone.' I answered the phone very guardedly. It was Leslie, but he sounded funny, and I could not believe it. He was shattered to have come thousands of miles and then have such an off-putting telephone conversation with what he had thought was his loving fiancée. He rang off and managed to get a taxi to bring him and his baggage (including a trunk full of wedding presents) to the H.Q. Meanwhile a kind friend said to me:

'Was it Leslie?'

I told him of my doubts, and reminded him of that coffee-break skit.

'Never mind. Let's get my car, and just go down and check at the bus station. The car's just parked round the corner.'

We went, and, as I suspected, no Leslie at the bus station. My companion said: 'Well, don't worry. I'll bring you down again later to meet the afternoon bus, if you really think today is the day.'

So back we went to the H.Q. He opened the gate for me, and there stood a bewildered Leslie, so I just ran into his arms while our Director stood on the steps above us and looked on with a satisfied grin. Later he interviewed us, and the question of just where we were to work as a translation team and with which language group came up. We would not be allocated until near the end of that year, but he gave us a short list of the language groups where he felt the need was most urgent at that time, with some suggested sources of further information on these peoples and places. Then he prayed with us.

Now the Mexican Branch of Wycliffe took us on as a special project, which seemed to be entitled, 'Get those English kids married'. Leslie had to leave to take his Jungle Camp training in a week's time, so everyone helped us plan and organise the wedding that would take place in three months' time, after his course at Jungle Camp. Those last few months of being near at hand, yet not seeing very much of each other, seemed much harder to us than the preceding two years had been. Letters and visits seemed too short and too far apart.

We arrived in Mexico City again one week before the wedding, and every time we started to do something, someone would come up and say:

'Can't I do that for you? You must have so much to do to get ready.'

We ended up with nothing to do, and when the Director heard that, he said: 'Blessings on you my children. Go out and be tourists — you'll never have another chance.'

In Mexico, the civil ceremony must be performed by the local judge before the church ceremony, so a senior worker was to take us round to see where the judge's office was, and to make an appointment with him for later in the week. He called us out of the baggage room where we were unpacking that trunk full of wedding presents, and said not to bother to change as he was just making the appointment. David and Margaret Bendor-Samuel emerged with us, equally dishevelled — although David, at least, was wearing a tie. They were to be our best man and matron of honour, so they thought they had better see where the office was too.

It turned out that the judge who was free would prefer to get it over with. Rather bemused, we all filed in, and the senior worker interpreted for us very briefly and informally, after the judge had read the appropriate Mexican laws and asked if we understood. He shook hands all round, we ordered four copies of the marriage certificate and left the office. As we stepped out of the door, a wedding party arrived by car — the bride resplendent in bridal attire, her bridesmaids, the groom and the witnesses, all dressed as they should be. Suddenly we realised how very untidy we were, and we left the scene quickly, smothering hysterical laughter. The senior worker was very pleased with himself at having got us married five days before the wedding day! Back at H.Q. he ushered us in for coffee-break:

'Ladies and gentlemen, may I present Mr. and Mrs. Leslie Pride.'

Everyone roared as they looked at our clothes.

'It's true,' he insisted, 'I just took them to the judge now.'

There were squeals of horror from the women, and the poor man backed out of the room with a grin, taking his coffee cup with him. Then they were convinced. As one person said:

'At least now you won't have to worry about what would be correct attire for a civil wedding in Mexico!'

We were deluged with presents and kindness during that week, and were quite overwhelmed by the generosity of our fellow Wycliffe workers. They were determined that it should be a thoroughly British wedding, but, of course, it turned out to be an absolutely marvellous cosmopolitan one with British, American and Mexican touches thoroughly mixed. Unbeknown to us, our fellow members had arranged a 'shower' party for us, and they had invited a number of other Christian friends as well. At the 'shower' a great bunch of balloons was lowered from the ceiling, and I was called upon to burst them one by one, and read out the note that I would find inside. Leslie was to carry out the instructions in the note. I was a bit reluctant, as I felt sure it was all a big joke, but I sat on the balloon, and read out the rhyme that I found, and Leslie set off on the mysterious errand indicated. Then, to my amazement, and everyone else's delight, he returned with an armful of presents. This was repeated, and we ended up with a ping-pong table full of presents — all sorts of useful household things like linen, towels, kitchen- and table-ware, and a beautiful miniature travelling iron. That was how we learnt what a 'shower' was — in fact, I was so overcome by everyone's love and generosity that I almost made it into a literal shower. Then next day the 'real' presents began to arrive including leather luggage and pillows. Then a sewing machine was delivered. This had been sent by my parents who, with great difficulty, had managed to arrange for it to be bought in Mexico. It was electric, but with a hand attachment, so that it could be converted when there was no electricity.

Another highlight was the trip to the flower market. Rows of skilled floral artists sat there making bouquets, wreaths and buttonholes, surrounded by banks of massed flowers of every hue. It was hard to decide both on the flowers, and on who should do it all, as vendors mobbed us with armloads of all kinds: roses or orchids? fresia or irises? gladioli or tube-roses for the church? Eventually we ordered yellow roses and carnations for my bouquet, and fresia with other flowers for Margaret's. We decided to leave the choice of flowers for the church and the reception to those gifted friends who were going to arrange them.

The church ceremony certainly went just as it was planned. It was rather special to have my Mexican friend Estela there with her parents, and also two car-loads of Otomí Indian friends. The Canadian of the coffee-break skit was very concerned about our parents missing all this, so he took over a hundred snaps of the proceedings, and had three copies made of each for our wedding present. That meant a complete set for each of our parents, and one for us.

The Directors had said to take a honeymoon, and then to live out in Mexico City, away from the H.Q., so that we had a chance to really get to know each other again while we did some Spanish study. We owe a lot to their kindness and understanding. They wanted us to take time too to find out just where in Mexico, and with which group of people, God wanted us to work. We had been given details of several places that were considered top priority, and of one or two others as well. It was also suggested that we should talk to several people who could tell us more about particular areas, peoples and languages. As we prayed, both of us were more and more drawn to the Chatino people in the county of Juquila, down in the south-west. Bill Upson had reported these constant rumours of the 'other Chatinos beyond the river', and was eager to go and locate them, and then to allocate a team there if necessary.

That was all it said on the Directors' list, so we went to

talk to Bill and Jay Upson. Bill played a Chatino tape for us to hear; it was just a jumble of sounds and glottal stops. We certainly would need a lot of help but what we heard about the people made us sure that these were the people to whom we should go. We started to plan the trip. We went out with the Upsons and bought what seemed like endless supplies (but then, it takes quite a lot to feed eight people for several months), packed them up, roped and banded the boxes and sent them off to Oaxaca City. Then we went on the bus ourselves, to Oaxaca City. After the all-night journey we were glad to transfer to a local bus for the final hour's drive to Mitla. Here we stayed at the small Translation Centre, and we were amazed by the contrasts we saw. Mitla is a rural Zapotec Indian town in a dry semi-desert valley. Because of their lack of arable land, the people have become very skilled textile craftsmen, and Mitla blankets, shawls, bags, etc. are greatly in demand, providing a good cash income for people who have to buy almost all their food. There are many little general stores and also an extensive market, as well as the craft shops and a textile market. Ruins from the ancient pre-conquest Zapotec civilisation have been excavated in the town, and are open to the public. This provides a big tourist attraction, so there is no lack of buyers for these beautiful hand-made goods.

The Missionary Aviation Fellowship also has a centre in Mitla. Bill and Jay had told us that they were able to fly to their county town of Juquila, and from there climb up the mountainside (usually on muleback) to their home in Yaitepec. Bill and Leslie saw the pilot to arrange a flight, checked out a two-way radio, collected our cargo from Oaxaca City, made a few last-minute purchases, sent a telegram to Juquila to arrange for mules, and then the great day dawned bright and clear. The Missionary Aviation Fellowship plane took us over four ranges of mountains and then down into a beautiful green valley, to land on a shelf carved out of the mountainside a hundred feet above the river. The Spanish-speaking friend in Juquila who had helped so many Wycliffe workers now came to meet us and to welcome Bill and Jay back again. He had received the telegram and arranged for mules. By the time we had all arrived with the basic cargo (the rest was labelled to come on later flights), an old Chatino friend had arrived with the mules. It had taken several flights, as the little M.A.F. plane could only carry a very limited amount, but now we said goodbye to the pilot, assuring him that we would establish radio contact as soon as possible, and off he went. The plane looked about the size of a yellow butterfly as it crawled up and clear of the mountains.

The cargo was loaded on to the mules, and the four Upson children were tied on to their mounts; then the adults mounted, and we were off. One-and-a-half hours later, and a thousand feet higher:

'There's our house,' said the eldest girl, and pointed to a whitewashed building on the side of the mountain. We went on past one or two others, and I looked at them curiously. These were big mud-brick houses, with red tile roofs, each house standing in its own grove of coffee bushes and clump of banana plants. Very different from the Zapotec houses in Mitla. Everywhere was green with luxuriant growth, and unlike Mitla, not a cactus in sight. These people too were obviously very different from the downtrodden Indians I had seen in some places, who owned so little. Everyone was amazed and delighted to see Bill and Jay, who because of furlough and ill health had not been there for more than two years.

We came to the house and unloaded. Then Bill went off to pay for the mules. They all belonged to one man, he said. I gasped, as I had never before met an Indian with more than one mule, and he was considered rich! From the porch in front of the house we could look many miles down the Juquila valley over seven little ridges.

'That's the way we'll go, Leslie, right down to the end, then across the Rio Verde to find those "other Chatinos". There are Chatinos all the way, and throughout these mountains on both sides,' said Bill. We wondered again where we would actually settle in the end.

We got ourselves organised for Christmas, and immediately afterwards the men set off. Jay and I wondered if we would really be able to manage that old radio, for which one had to crank the generator with bicycle pedals, and talk into the microphone at the same time. I 'rode the bicycle' and Jay talked, and it worked quite well, to our surprise.

We had worked out a routine whereby Jay taught the children their school-work in the mornings, while I went to visit our next-door neighbour, Tema. She supplied our daily tortillas, and Jay had asked her to teach me to make tortillas too. She was a little shocked to meet a married woman who could not make tortillas — How did I feed my husband? Did he know my shortcomings before we were married? — but she was quite happy to teach me. She spoke no Spanish at all, so we knew that I would learn some Chatino at the same time as learning her domestic art. Bill and Leslie had done some visiting in the town, where Bill had asked lots of questions, and Leslie had been able to observe something of Chatino family life. Now that the men had gone, Jay and I continued our routine, and I took the children off her hands for an hour or so in the afternoons, with nature walks, sewing, and so on.

Ten days later, Bill and Leslie came home both saddle-worn and foot-sore. They needed sleep too, but they had an exciting tale to tell of their adventures and their reception in the various places. Yes, there was more than one Chatino language all right — not two, but three. Bill had been happily able to communicate as far as Tepenixtlahuaca, and then came Tataltepec:

'It's at the very end of this Juquila valley,' he said pointing, 'beyond that furthest hazy ridge.'

Here they had found a warm welcome and a new language, but they had not come to the Rio Verde yet, so they went on. Up and up the mountain ridge on the very rough Santa

María trail. Then, down from Santa María to the river crossing with the *maroma*.

'What's a *maroma*, Daddy?'

'Well, there's this big thick rope slung across the river, and then there are rope circles hung on it. You sit in one and go sliding down to the middle of the river. Then you pull yourself up the other side by the main rope. Uncle Leslie took a photo of me, so you'll be able to see it when it's developed.'

Later that day they had come to Zenzontepec, and were given an even warmer welcome, but it was another new language. There were a few Spanish speakers there, although most of the population were Chatinos. One bilingual man on the town council was very eager to hear why they had come. When he heard about the intention to translate the Bible into Chatino, he was eager to hear more, and Bill witnessed to him from his Spanish Bible for some hours. Everyone seemed to like the idea of books in Chatino, and they liked even more the idea that we would help them to build a town airstrip, as they desperately wanted better communication with Oaxaca City for their own political reasons. So they extended an invitation to Leslie to return with me to live in Zenzontepec and learn the language.

This was encouraging news to all four of us, and we began to plan. As one of the children needed dental attention, Bill decided to take her to Mitla immediately after the birthday of her brother, Charles. When she returned, the plane would take us to Mitla to join Bill and buy a few personal supplies. It seemed a good plan, and we looked forward to little Charles's fourth birthday.

However, on that day I became quite ill. Bill and the little girl left the next day as planned, but I was no better. One day in the following week, the pilot told us that he would come the next day. I was up again now, but very dizzy and weak, and Leslie was unwell too, so Jay suggested that the pilot bring Bill back with their daughter, and take us out to the doctor. Then we could let them know by radio when we were better, so that Bill could come with us to Zenzontepec.

We usually walked down the mountain to the plane and rode up, but the next morning both Leslie and I were slumped on the backs of our mules, and very grateful for those Mexican saddles with the big pommel to hang on to. We did not attempt to hold the reins.

Back at the centre in Mitla, kind fellow-workers looked after us, and took us to see the doctor. Bacillary dysentery for Leslie and paratyphoid for me — it seemed such a set-back after the excitement of the survey trip and planning.

After a month's convalescence we were ready to start again. Bill came, and on March 1st, two Wycliffe friends took us, the radio and our stuff, to the end of the dirt road, which was as near as we could get to Zenzontepec by road. The rest could only be done by footpath. Bill managed to arrange for mules, and the next day we loaded up and set off. It turned out that our guide did not know the trail very well, so he was very relieved when he recognised the Santiago Minas valley and turned up it. We were not too sorry to say goodbye to him when we had found a place to spend the night. We were to sleep at one end of a lady's porch. A card-party went on at the other end till well after midnight, and she and her family barred themselves inside the house for the night. We had supper, put our big groundsheet down on the earth floor, blew up the air-mattresses, crawled into sleeping bags and I slept. I was nearest the wall, then Leslie, then Bill — nearest to the card-players. The men were restless, but I didn't even hear those drunks leave. I had thought it rather cissy to get out the air-mattresses on the trail, but after an unaccustomed day in the saddle, I was very grateful for that cushion of air between me and the ground!

First thing next morning, Angel, our new guide, appeared with a new lot of mules. He had been summoned by our hostess, and he assured us that he most certainly knew every centimetre of the trail to Zenzontepec, and he would come all the way with us, even though it was two days' journey. After haggling over the cost, we had coffee and were off.

Breakfast comes later in Mexico, and it made a welcome break at some village on the way. That night we stayed at a lonely house on the Rio Limón. They obviously had very little, but the woman hurried to make a meal for us, and seemed so pleased to have company. Drinking water was always a problem on the trail, but she boiled our water-bottles in the top of her great pot of bubbling maize corn that was tomorrow's bread supply. She could not quite understand why we wanted to drink cold cooked water — what was wrong with the river or streams along the way? — but she willingly cooperated when she discovered that we did want it. At bed-time, she saw Bill reading his New Testament, and wanted to know what it was and what it said. He brought out his Spanish version, and they talked long into the night. Although very conscious of our own lack of Spanish, we were thrilled by Bill's opportunity, and went to sleep wondering how long it would be before the Chatinos had a New Testament in their language, so that the same sort of encounter would be possible with one of them as tonight with this Spanish speaker.

We had all helped shuck corn for the mules the night before, so at dawn Angel was up to catch and feed them. We had coffee, and the woman was almost in tears as she waved goodbye and we rode off. Mule travel had become routine now. The first day, we had noticed every plant and bird, exclaimed over the flowers, and kept up a constant conversation about all that we saw. By the third day, Leslie and Bill were playing their brand of traveller's chess. Each one made three moves at a time. Then, the one in front leaned back over his mule's tail, and the one behind leaned forward over his mule's ears, to exchange the set. It was a good thing the pieces stood in close-fitting holes! Angel was most intrigued by these antics and begged to be taught the game, so each time we stopped for a meal, Bill and Leslie instructed him while we waited for the food to be cooked. It was a new experience on that trip to enquire at a house if they could serve us a meal, and then to see our hostess, or perhaps her daughter, run outside to catch and kill a hen, which was then prepared for us to eat.

We came over the pass into a dry, rather barren valley, with steep sides falling down to the river at the bottom, where a narrow band of irrigated land contrasted richly with the surrounding infertile valley. The trail stretched away into the distance as a scratch on the mountainside leading down to the river ford. On the opposite side of the valley was tier upon tier of small thatched houses with a few bigger adobe mud-brick ones in the middle. Zenzontepec at last! We could see the trail climb up the mountainside from the ford. We could hear the loudspeakers blaring out records of pop music, and Bill consulted Angel. Sure enough, we had chosen an important town fiesta day for our arrival — number one in the 'what-not-to-do-when-arriving-at-a-new-allocation' list! We were made welcome notwithstanding, when we eventually arrived in the town square and slid wearily from the backs of our mules; but the town authorities were physically quite unfit to see us at that time. One semi-sober official waved us genially to the half-finished new teachers' house on the square, and there we camped for the night.

I was excited. So this was Zenzontepec, where we were to live and work. We could hear Chatino being spoken all round us, but we could not understand a word. With all his experience of the Yaitepec area, and his knowledge of the Chatino language spoken there, Bill couldn't understand it either. We knew that what we had learnt in Yaitepec, and all that had been written about that language, would stand us in good stead, but we also knew that we were going to have to start from scratch.

In the morning, a town messenger appeared, complete with a little stick that marked his office, and told Bill and Leslie that the town president would like to see them now at the Town Hall. They went and were cordially welcomed, then conducted to a little house higher up the hill. It had been used by a schoolteacher but was now unoccupied. We would be welcome to stay there for the time being. So we moved up the hill to our new home, and began to make friends with the neighbours. The authorities had apologised for the lack of a kitchen, but they had no objection to us building one on. Meantime, it was the dry season, and Bill managed to buy a load of firewood from someone, so I lit my cooking fire outside between three large stones. We had carefully packed the lid of a small oil drum in our baggage, and this made a very good hot-plate. We bought eggs from a neighbour, dried meat from another neighbour, tortillas from another, and flour, rice, onions, sugar, salt, soap powder and tinned sardines from a general store just down the hill. After a home-cooked meal Bill and Leslie set about fixing up the aerial so that we could get in radio contact with the centre.

Then, 'X-45, X-45, X-45 from X-21. Can you hear me?'

'X-21 from X-45. I hear you loud and clear. How are you? Do you have any message?'

'X-45 from X-21. Only that we arrived without trouble, and the authorities have given the Prides permission to live here. Till tomorrow.'

'Until tomorrow, X-21. X-45 retiring from the air.'

It was good to hear the pilot's voice, even if the conversation was all in Spanish. It is amazing what a sense of security and not-aloneness that radio link always gives. This kind of communication was astounding to our neighbours, of course. A few of the richer ones had little transistor radios, and one or two of the more sophisticated, who had travelled out to the state capital, had seen a telephone used, but a two-way radio was completely new.

Leslie and Bill were soon called to the Town Hall again. The authorities were very impressed to hear about the communications radio, and immediately saw its usefulness with regard to the project that they had in mind. Would the señores please come up and inspect their work on the airstrip? They needed advice about its construction, since they had never done anything like that before, and having seen it, could they talk to the Señor Piloto about it, to get his expert opinion, and ask him if he would come and try it out? So the next day saw us, accompanied by the official in charge of public work, and a lot of townspeople, making our way down to a tributary of the river and up the other side to a little ridge that stuck out from the side of the mountain. There was a small natural meadow on it which sloped fairly steeply, and this was the potential airstrip. Bill and Leslie paced out length and width, and examined the actual surface. Then they said that they thought it might just do if a lump was smoothed out at the approach, as every available metre would need to be used for landing. Upon our return, the authorities all came up to our house to hear the conversation with the pilot.

For five days we basked in the good graces of the people of Zenzontepec, and then things changed. Our neighbours' attitude became more guarded, the authorities more evasive. The town council member who had first questioned Bill eagerly about the Bible during the survey trip remained friendly, and came to tell us that the people were being stirred up against us for political reasons. When I went to wash our clothes in the stream, the other women moved away and did their washing at a safe distance. When I went to the spring for water, the other women kept away. I walked casually down a trail, and a child that had been shyly friendly the day before ran screaming to his mother, and hid in her skirts. Then a campaign began on the town loud-speaker, telling everyone to avoid us, not to be friendly, and not to sell us anything to eat, so that we would go away. In spite of all this, the official in charge of public works was still eager to get the airstrip opened. The day arrived when it had been arranged that the pilot was to come and try it out. We could not explain the change of feeling over the radio, so Bill just warned the pilot to reconnoitre the strip very carefully before attempting a landing, and then the procession set out for the airstrip to meet him there. It was quite impossible for him to land as tree trunks had been dragged into position all over the strip as deliberate obstacles. The official in charge of public work was furious, but when he rounded on his fellow councillors he got no cooperation, just avoidance answers to his imperious questions. Our gloom was lifted by a little packet of letters that the pilot dropped to us on a little parachute, plus a hastily scribbled note from himself, written as he circled above us over the strip:

'Seems like someone doesn't want you there. We'll be praying back at the centre.'

This was encouraging, and so were the letters, as the ones we had received through the local postal service appeared to have been opened.

A few days later, Leslie decided to go out and cut some poles for the legs of a mud-stove. Since all the Chatino people now seemed afraid of us, which meant that our language learning was at a stand-still, he thought this would be a good way to use the time. Also he was spurred on by the sight of two holes burnt in my skirt from squatting on the ground by the fire to cook each meal. While he was gone, a town messenger appeared, and ordered Bill to appear before the president at the Town Hall immediately. Bill grabbed up our credentials and went with him, but after an hour I began to wonder what was happening. Then Leslie returned with four beautiful, straight, sturdy poles, exactly right for the stove legs. Later on we saw Bill coming slowly up the path.

'Well, they really gave me a grilling,' he said. 'They wanted to know who we were working for, why we were here, and so on again and again. I see you got the legs for the stove, Leslie. That was a nice straight tree if you got all four poles from the one — what was it anyway? Where did you find it?'

'Oh, there's a little bit of irrigated land just round that shoulder of the mountain, and there are a few bushes and trees around it. Actually, a man appeared after I had cut it, and kept saying something to me, but I couldn't understand him. I think he followed me back into town. What is *aguacate*, Bill?'

'Is that what he said? Oh, no! Are you sure? How could you?'

Thoroughly bewildered, Leslie asked him, 'How could I, what?'

'You just cut down somebody's avocado pear tree for the stove legs. You couldn't have done it at a worse time, as they have become so suspicious of us. Come on, we had better go back to the Town Hall right away, and confess, and pay up the fine.'

Leslie, thoroughly crestfallen, muttered, 'But it was a lovely straight trunk just the right thickness, and the tree wasn't inside a fence or anything . . .'

They arrived at the Town Hall just as the man who had followed Leslie finished reporting the incident to an incredulous town council. Bill now apologised profusely and explained that Leslie had had no idea that the tree belonged to anyone, and certainly not that it was an avocado pear tree, since they did not grow in his home country. The council were at first amazed, and then with one accord burst out laughing. The idea that anyone in the world could mistake an avocado tree for building material, and not know that it had an owner, was quite beyond them. Meanwhile, the owner had been called, and a figure was amicably agreed on for his compensation, which Leslie paid on the spot. He and Bill left the council chamber still buzzing over the phenomenon of such ignorance in the world, and they came home to dinner feeling that the air had been cleared a little by this joke on us.

'Leslie, I would never have advised you to cut down someone's avocado tree, but just maybe you did the best possible thing in this crazy situation,' said Bill.

One evening, the really friendly councillor came to visit us. He brought us eggs and bananas, which were very welcome, now that everyone was afraid to let us have any supplies.

'Various stories have been started about you such as that you eat little children — but the most damaging is that you are in league with our enemies in the town next to us. We are in the middle of a land war with them. Some people have already been killed by the other side who thought they were trespassing. A few of us really want you to stay, but most people are very afraid, and I think the council will ask you officially to leave.' Then he asked more questions about the Scriptures.

It was a thrill in the middle of all this anti-feeling and intrigue to have this one man really eager to know the truth of God. It was also a thrill to see that gift of eggs and bananas, which almost had me in tears of gratitude as I considered our larder. Never before had I needed to pray, 'Give us this day today's food' because I had none.

That night we were awakened by a great scurrying, pattering, and plop! Then silence. We turned over and went to sleep again. We should have got up to investigate! Mice had been rushing round the top of our mud-brick wall, and leaping across the corner as a shortcut. One did not quite manage it, and it fell into my clay pot of boiled water that was cooling. I boiled the pot and scrubbed it, and boiled it again with soap, but the smell and taste of that drowned mouse body would not leave it, so I broke that precious water-pot, and threw it away, even though I knew that no one would sell us another.

Soon came the official request that we should leave. We were so glad to have that radio link so that we could consult our director, and to know of the prayers of our fellow workers. In desperation we resorted to English to describe the situation to him, and he felt that we would gain nothing by remaining at that time when such feeling had been generated against us. So Bill and Leslie made one more trip down the hill to the Town Hall, and told them that we would leave if that was what they really wanted. The people were so thoroughly afraid of us by now that no one would hire out his animals for our use, and in the end town messengers were sent to a Spanish-speaking village four hours journey away to get the animals.

Exactly three weeks after our excited arrival, we

disappointedly left that isolated town of Chatinos 'beyond the river', forced to believe that Zenzontepec was not the Lord's place for us after all, that it was not His time. Where were we supposed to settle, then? We had felt so sure of God's leading, but something had gone wrong somewhere — or what was the purpose of it all?

3

The Mountain People

THREE DAYS ON the trail again, but this time we didn't have to worry about fresh animals as the Zenzontepec beasts were to go with us all the way. Three town messengers who could speak some Spanish came with us: two to look after the animals and return them afterwards, and the third, a younger fellow, to carry the radio on his back because there weren't enough animals. We started late and made slow progress as one of the animals was both ancient and sickly. Night came on, and we didn't seem to have arrived anywhere.

'That's the Rio Limón down there,' the Zenzontepec men told us.

So we plunged down the steep mountainside, and eventually came out on the river bank, glad to see the moon again after the dark shadows under the trees. After splashing along in the shallows for a bit, we eventually came to a clearing that we recognised, but it was now about nine p.m. and all was dark and still. We moved forward up the bank, and then pandemonium broke loose as the dogs started to bark and rushed out to the attack. The Zenzontepec men had armed themselves with stones from the river bank, and now threw them at the dogs accurately (judging by the yelps of pain) and methodically, holding their ground in spite of those snapping, snarling hounds. I was rather glad that I was still mounted! The family soon roused, and while the husband called off the dogs, the friendly woman came to welcome us and, in spite of the inconvenience, seemed delighted to see us again. She quickly blew up her kitchen fire and made us all some supper while her husband helped the men with the mules. She remembered that we had boiled the water-bottles before, so she asked us for them, filled them up and boiled the water for us as we were eating. Then she came over to talk to Bill again about the Scriptures. It was such a thrill to meet this interest after all that had happened in the last three weeks.

We left again in the morning, rested, refreshed and at peace, sure that God was in control and quite able to cope with all the seeming setbacks, even though we didn't understand what was going on. From the Rio Limón we now took the trail towards Yaitepec and home. At about midday we crossed the Rio Verde — the 'Big River' in Chatino thinking — and from then on the Zenzontepec men were very unsure of themselves. They knew that they were now out of their own area; they could no longer communicate in their own language, and they were afraid. Suddenly we were the only people that they knew, and they were looking to us for friendship and protection.

By contrast, we were glad to see the 'Big River' and the pine trees on the horizon far above us, heralding the much more fertile, lush and green, Juquila Valley on the other side. There was a narrow strip of irrigated land by the river, then a dry, open trail, with thorn bushes and cactus as the commonest vegetation among the rocks. Hour after hour we climbed up the mountainside. We saw the vegetation change as we got higher. Then came the scrub oaks festooned with Spanish moss and decorated with beautiful orchids and bromeliads, and we were so glad of the shade. It was getting dark and the place we wanted to reach was still high above us. Suddenly, that ancient, sickly pack animal groaned, sighed, and sank to the ground. They couldn't manage to get it on its feet again, so Bill suggested that we make camp in the open when we came to the little stream in a natural pasture that he knew was nearby. We left the beast and went on. Soon we could hear the stream, and the men quickly unloaded and unsaddled all the animals except the strongest. Bill and one of the others took that one back to get the pack from the spent animal, while Leslie and the other two found some firewood and got a fire going. I rummaged in our belongings and found some packets of soup and a pot to cook it in. We still had some coffee too, and I heated water for that. The Zenzontepec men were amazed when Bill offered them some soup — they had philosophically started munching on the dry tortillas that they carried, and had got out their gourd bowls to scoop up a drink of water from the stream. Now they were glad to have the hot soup in their bowls, and wanted to share their tortillas with us. They were even more amazed when Bill said:

'It is our custom to thank God for our food and for His help on the trail.' Then he prayed in Spanish.

On up to the top of the pass the next morning and through the town of San Juan. It was heart-warming to respond to friendly Chatino greetings as people recognised Bill, and to actually understand some of what people were saying. We waited while Bill was rushed off to see someone who was ill, but there was nothing he could do as the patient appeared to have tuberculosis. He explained that this illness needed lots of medicine for a long time, and that if they could possibly take the patient to Oaxaca City to see a government doctor it would be best. While we were waiting for Bill, I suddenly noticed our companions. They were standing as near to us as possible, with their backs to the local people. Occasionally they muttered to each other, but their faces were tense and scared. They were very glad when we started down the mountain again.

In the afternoon we struggled up the now familiar trail from Juquila to Yaitepec. The ancient, sickly animal had no pack today as we did not want it to die before they got it back home, so its pack was on Leslie's beast, and we took turns to walk.

We came to the top and looked across to the house.

'Home, sweet home. And will I be glad to get there!' said Bill, then waved his hat and whistled as he noticed a child in the garden. The next minute all four Upson children knew that Dad was coming and had erupted from the house to tear down the trail to meet him. Jay appeared on the porch and waved, and no doubt counted how many of us were coming.

'That was my wife,' said Bill to our companions. 'This is Yaitepec, and that is my home that I told you about. These are my children coming now.' We let the children ride the mules that last little bit, and Bill replied to the friendly Chatino enquiries sung out from the houses along the way, and then we arrived.

One of the Zenzontepec men looked wonderingly at Bill and said: 'So you really were telling the truth all the time!'

This was a shock to all of us, but Bill quickly recovered and said, 'I hope you will tell that to everyone back in your home town, but you can learn about us from anyone here in Yaitepec. Why don't you ask these people what we do here?'

'Us? talk to the Chatinos of Yaitepec? But they are murderers and always carry guns. They would kill us if they knew we had come from beyond the river.'

'As you like,' said Bill in reply, 'but they are all good friends of ours. Aren't you coming with me to buy some corn and fodder for the animals? I can't carry it all.'

At that point Jay called us all in to coffee and cake with the promise of a slap-up meal a little later. Cake was quite new to our companions, but they enjoyed it too after they recovered from their trepidation at entering the house. Then they decided that they would all go with Bill to get food for the animals — safety in numbers, I suppose. Later they were amazed that Jay served us all together at the table and that we had familiar tortillas, rice, black beans, cooking bananas and beef. We don't know what they said when they got home, but we do know that the malicious rumours about us persisted.

It seemed wisest to remain in Yaitepec for the present, so next day I went back to see Tema again to continue my interrupted tortilla-making lessons. She wanted to know if we were going to stay now, and did we want a house? I said that we did, and when I returned home later I found that her brother had already been to offer his big main room for rent, and Bill and Leslie had more or less arranged the matter, but were just waiting for me so that we could all go and inspect the place. There it was, an adobe mud-brick house, with a wide porch running the length of the large room and a small window with wooden shutters. There was a separate door into the smaller room at the end where the four teenage sons slept, and also a small archway between the two rooms. We had an earth floor, and the room was furnished with two long, very narrow, benches, one chair, and the family altar, with some wooden crosses planted beneath it. No, they would not need to use the altar, the owner said; Granny might come in and put flowers on it occasionally, but only if we were at home. There was only one day that they would need to come to it, but the ceremony would not take very long, and we need take no notice they assured us. We discussed the kitchen which I was to set up on the porch, and our landlord said that he would go and cut poles for a mud stove right away. We were very glad of his offer — at least no more avocado trees would get cut down this way, and if we were to move in that afternoon, Leslie would not have time to cut poles anyway.

The next day we built the mud stove, incorporating our same old, trusty, oil drum lid as the hot plate, and some old tin cans fitted together made a good chimney. Our landlord had also brought us a load of firewood, so the stove was soon in use. They sold us some of their wild bamboo poles, and with these we made a four-tier set of shelves suspended from the rafters on ropes. The air-mattresses and sleeping bags came into use again for our bed, and the children watched with wondering eyes as we blew them up, then they rushed off to report. Soon Granny arrived on a state visit with some bananas for a present. After a little it transpired that she really wanted to try out our bed. Soon the whole family were sitting on it and exclaiming how soft air is! They admired the shelves, then crossed the yard to their own kitchen and, no doubt, discussed the peculiarities of the foreigners. Obviously we were going to get plenty of language practice.

We placed our folding table right by the window so that we could get the maximum light when using it, and we were very glad of the one chair that came with the room. Apart from that, we had a small drum of paraffin to keep our Tilley lamp going, and a large wooden chest with a hinged lid, so we were quite well off for seats. We used the window as a convenient hatch to the kitchen, and with this arrangement it was quite obvious to any passer-by when we were having meals. The children next door came the next morning and they watched me cook the dinner with great interest. Finally I passed everything through and went inside for the meal. They stayed on the porch, and were just peeping through the window when a wrathful voice bellowed out from the kitchen across the way. Our landlord, Lauro, emerged from his kitchen door, obviously in the middle of his own meal, and verbally tore the children to shreds. They ran away frightened, and he retired again.

Later, when he was sure that we had finished because I was outside washing up he came over to visit us. Then he told us:

'You mustn't let children watch while you are eating. That's terribly bad manners. I don't know what their parents are thinking of, but Chatinos just don't do that, so when you are ready to eat, just tell them plainly, and make sure they leave, and if one of my boys does it, you just let me know, because I won't have it. Another thing, when you need firewood, just let me know and I'll bring a load in from the cornfield. Oh yes, and don't be afraid about that archway to the boys' room. Now that you've put the curtain no one will ever come through it, I guarantee that. Just tell me if anything is not right, because you live with my family now. Do you want to write down some Chatino now, Leslie, because

I'm not going out again this afternoon? The boys can manage alone, so I can help you if you like.'

Yes, we were really accepted into that family, yet they never came into our room without being invited. However, as soon as our light went out at nights we would hear from the boys' room:

'Leslie, Leslie, are you asleep?'

'No, but I want to go to sleep.'

'Leslie, are you coming to work with us in the cornfield tomorrow?'

'I'll see. What time will you go?'

'Oh, long before breakfast — you won't be awake!' Stifled giggles, then 'Let's go to sleep now. Good night.'

'Good night, then.'

In fact, only occasionally did that family go off to work before breakfast, but Rodi, Beto and Juan thought this nightly conversation a great joke, and took it in turns to initiate it. After a few days, Leslie decided that it would be good language practice and a good opportunity to be with the men of the family if he did go out to the cornfield with them. So, that night:

'Leslie, Leslie, are you asleep?' said Rodi.

'Yes, because I need to sleep so that I have strength to come to the cornfield with you tomorrow.'

'Will you really come to work with us, then?'

'Yes, I'm coming with you tomorrow.'

'Would you like me to sharpen your matchet really well for you in the morning so that you can help us cut?' from Juan.

'Yes, please. Good night, then.'

'We'll all eat breakfast first. Good night, Leslie,' from Rodi.

As soon as we opened our window and door in the morning, Juan rushed over to enquire if Leslie had really meant it, and excitedly bore off his matchet to be sharpened. It came back like a razor, and I was glad that Leslie had a leather scabbard for it. Most of the Chatinos nonchalantly carried their bare matchets over their forearms. I do not think much work was done that first morning, but Leslie learnt a great deal from Lauro, while Rodi and his brothers let off their high spirits by rolling great boulders down through the cornfield so that they went hurtling on into the valley below. This was not difficult, as their cornfield was on a very steep mountainside, and the rock once dislodged could crash on down for perhaps a thousand feet without too much impediment. They did bring back some firewood from this expedition, and Lauro and his sons seemed to be very proud of their new protégé.

Meanwhile I continued to work with Tema. One day she decided that it was time I learnt to count. So she taught me the numbers one to two thousand, and made sure that I wrote them all down. As I took down seemingly endless numbers, I wondered, where, oh where, were these languages that have only the numbers one to three in their system? I had learnt about them in the linguistics courses, but Chatino was obviously not one of them.

We often spent time with Bill and Jay, picking their brains to help us sort out what we had written down, and to discuss the customs that we were observing all the time. But Bill was being troubled by a pain in his back. As the pain became more severe he was unable to do much practical work and even desk work was limited. We suddenly realised the import of this when Leslie met Jay carrying two big buckets of water up to the house from the spring. She sent the children down with their little buckets, but it just was not enough for a family of six; so Leslie tried to keep an eye on their water buckets too, but it was hard to do it tactfully, and we weren't always aware of their need.

One night we were both suddenly awake and aware of someone in the room. A light was moving towards us, but no one spoke. Feigning sleep, we saw Granny place a lighted candle on the altar table, then slip out through the curtain. Leslie looked at his watch — three a.m. — so we turned over and went back to sleep by candlelight. Some time later,

Granny came again and replaced the guttering candle. We had just dozed off once more when she came back yet again, so we woke up thoroughly and found that it was five-thirty a.m. We decided that we had better get up; this must be the fiesta to which Lauro had referred. We could hear muffled scuffles and whispers in the boys' room, so Leslie hopped out of bed to light the lamp, and I sat up and reached for my clothes. He was in his pyjamas and was watching the heating-up process of lighting a Tilley lamp, while I had got as far as my blouse — no skirt — when the entire family filed in. I stayed sitting in the sleeping bag, and Lauro said:

'Good morning. Please excuse us, but today we have a special custom for this fiesta of the Holy Cross, and every family must pay respect to their crosses.'

'Please carry on,' said Leslie, 'don't mind us.'

Lauro was carrying a large white lighted candle with which he lit the candles carried by the others, then they all flopped to their knees and crawled forwards, holding the lighted candles before them. When they got to the altar table, Lauro and Granny stood up and stood their candles on the table, but everyone else planted theirs near the crosses underneath. Then they all stood up, politely said 'We're going now', put their hats on and left. From time to time throughout the morning Granny came in to see if Lauro's big candle was still burning and standing upright, and she brought some hibiscus to decorate the altar table, but no further reference was made to the event.

We noticed that everyone was wearing his best clothes, and no one went out to work that day. In the afternoon Granny suddenly appeared and walked right in. She was carrying a rifle, and thrust it into Leslie's hands saying, 'Please hide this. They say he's drunk.' Next we saw Lauro's wife, Pescasia, tying the three-year-old on her back in her shawl, then she softly but urgently called the next two, the ten- and twelve-year-olds, to come with her, and ran off down the trail. The teenagers were out somewhere, and Granny was in the kitchen. Then Lauro appeared, lurching down the trail to his house, and very drunk. He called out for his eldest son, Rodi, and accused him of all sorts of horrible things:

'He's no real son of mine. I'll kill him,' he said, and went into the kitchen and on to his bedroom, looking for his gun. Granny tried to distract him, but was thrown out of the way. Then she tried to make him eat something, but he got very angry and shouted out anything obscene that came into his head. The gun was not there, so he looked for his matchet, but this was not to be found either, so he started throwing plates and pots on the ground. Then he picked up the axe and came over to the boys' room. We were very glad that no one was there, but Granny had not checked that room, and he found one the boys' razor sharp matchets. He dropped the axe and picked up the matchet, then stumbled off down the trail waving the matchet and shouting for his son's blood. Granny quickly ran over to us and said: 'Don't be afraid. It is only Rodi that he hates — he won't hurt anyone else. Please keep the gun till I come for it.'

We and Granny were the only ones at home that night. The boys turned up for breakfast in the morning, and Lauro returned rather dishevelled and somewhat shamefaced, looking for a meal, about dinner time. He spoke to his sons quite normally and we wondered if we had misunderstood, and it was someone else that he wanted to kill when drunk. Pescasia returned with the little ones in the afternoon after she had ascertained that her husband was now quite sober. Not till the men had drifted off again on various errands did Granny come for the gun. 'He will want it tomorrow when he goes to the cornfield,' was all she said.

In May the cornfields are burnt off. All the bushes and trees have been cut down and left to dry out. Now they are burnt in readiness for planting with the first rains. At that time of year as a herald of the rainy season a thick fog rolls in like a blanket every afternoon, smothering everything in dampness. This dampness accentuated Bill's pain, and they decided to leave by mid-May, but, of course, all the packing up fell to Jay. We helped where we could, but it was not easy, although we were able to occupy the four lively children for some of the time. We were very sorry to see them go, but glad that they would now get medical help from the doctor. Smoke from the burning cornfields had made visibility very bad for the pilot, so that on some days flying was impossible, but we knew that they left on the day that the Lord had planned for their departure, because the pilot reported bright, clear weather, and he would be on his way in five minutes. We rushed to get Bill and a couple of children mounted, plus one mule-load of baggage for that first flight, and off they went, with Leslie to look after the animals. Jay and I finished getting the rest of the baggage ready for the muleteer to load, and then started on the anti-rat precautions. We filled their two tin trunks with clothes and bedclothes; we hung other edible (by rats) things from the rafters in rope bags on wire hooks (rats can run up and down ropes); we were just melting candles on the stove, to pour wax on the top of all the storage biscuit tins, when we heard the plane. It was time to go, and I assured Jay that I could finish up for her — I now knew what I would need to do in a few weeks' time. Then Jay and the children were mounted, and off they went with the muleteer, not knowing if they would ever come back.

I finished waxing the tins, disconnected the calor gas from the stove, checked round the house once more, and secured the remaining window shutters. I had heard the plane come back, so now I quickly locked the door and stood outside. It circled round over Yaitepec to gain altitude, and I waved a last goodbye. The plane waggled its wings in acknowledgment, and then they were gone over the pass. I hurried home to make some dinner as Leslie would be back in another hour and I needed to light the fire first. That afternoon Lauro and Granny both came over to see us at different times, and to reassure us that we must not be sad because Bill and Jay had gone. They assured us that they were glad we were staying, and they would look after us. One or two other friends came too with little presents of food and reassurance. We were touched to see their friendliness and thoughtfulness for us.

On May 25th everyone was very excited. This was a very important fiesta because St. James, the patron saint of Yaitepec — who in their beliefs has carried on the traditional function of rain god — was to be brought back into the church from his booth out on the mountainside. Then the rainy season would begin and the maize could be planted. The procession left with candles, and all the women carried little home-made clay censers with incense burning in them. When they returned, Granny brought Lauro's gun over to us for safe-keeping once more. Leslie checked and sure enough it was loaded, so he unloaded it before hiding it under our mattress.

Once more, Lauro lurched home drunk in the afternoon, but he was not fighting mad this time, just sleepy, so he went to bed and we heard no more of it.

Then the rains came. We had never seen anything like this before. A tremendous tropical storm, with ear-splitting cracks of thunder reverberating through the mountains. A strange, dark, purplish light came over everything, and then the rain fell. It just streamed down, not like rain drops or streaks, but like millions of taps turned on full. It fell down vertically, and above the din as it pounded on the tile roofs Lauro called across the yard: 'Be ready to put something under any leaks, because the tiles walk in the earth tremors.'

We rushed inside and put a bucket under a thin stream cascading down near the door, but none of our things were getting wet. All our clothes and papers were stored in large plastic bags on the shelves because of the dampness. We were glad of this precaution now, as there was no further need to worry about them.

By evening the rain had stopped, and next morning everywhere was bright and clear — all the smoke washed away, all the trees and undergrowth fresh and clean, and the earth soaked.

'One more rain like that and we can plant' said Lauro. 'Everywhere the earth must be thoroughly wet to the depth of my fingers before we plant the corn.'

It rained again and they went out to plant. They took the specially pointed planting sticks, and the special seed gourds with a square hole cut in the side and a string to hang round the neck. Plunge in the stick, drop five kernels of maize in the hole and one bean, kick the earth in with your heel, and move forward a pace diagonally up the mountainside. In a few days the shoots are through, and then the field must be watched to keep off mischievous wild marauders.

But now we had to leave for a few months as we had been asked to help with the training of new members. Bill and Jay had written to say that they were returning to the U.S.A. for an early and extended furlough, so would we like to use their house in the meantime? We packed everything up securely and stored it in their house, and then we said goodbye and were on our way down the now-familiar trail to the airstrip.

4

Yaitepec

THAT SUMMER WE had the opportunity to buy a tape-recorder at a discount. A tape-recorder was still a very expensive item at the time, but we knew that we really needed it, so we wrote to the finance office to enquire about the state of our account. If we have this much money in our account, please send us a cheque, we said. A letter came back by return with the cheque, and we praised the Lord and gratefully bought the tape-recorder. When we got back to Mexico City after the summer's study, we discovered that it had all been a mistake, and we were now deeply in debt. This really rocked us as neither of us had ever been in debt before, and perhaps we had been a bit smug about it. Now, we realised that it is possible to get into debt quite unwittingly, but still we could not understand it.

In Wycliffe our income all comes from donations. Those that are designated for a particular person or project are forwarded by the home office to that person or project. But many donors send gifts which are not specifically designated. Such money is put into the Emergency Fund, which is divided each month among those workers with the lowest income compared to their actual need — determined by the local cost of living, work and travel expenses, and other projects. To provide finance for the administration of the organisation, we each pay ten per cent of our income — half goes to run the home office, and half to the field office. This all means that we do not know just how much money we have received until we get our statement of accounts from our field office each month.

We had told the Lord that we would only take advantage of this opportunity to buy a tape recorder at a discount if we had the money. We had written to the office and asked, and had been reassured that it was there, so we had used the cheque. No one knew quite how the mistake had been made — what shall we do, Lord? Almost in tears we went to see the Director, and he was very sympathetic, and assured us that the office finances could stand this loan to cover our deficit until we had repaid it little by little. Meantime, he said we should hurry back to Yaitepec, and push ahead learning Chatino, since it looked as if we were going to have to take over the Upsons work after all, if the mountain people were ever to have any Scripture in their own language.

'But how can we? We haven't a penny to buy supplies with, and what about the bus fare, and then the M.A.F. flight?'

'Well, the office will just have to increase the loan for the moment.'

'But we can't just get more and more into debt!'

'Look, it costs more for us to subsidise you to live here in Mexico City than it does out in Yaitepec. Also, out there you are getting on with the job, but here you would just be filling in time, because I have no particular job for you to do here. There is money already given to the Lord for you somewhere between here and the donors, so just get on with your job earning that income, and don't worry about the debt. Do you think the Lord doesn't know about that financial "mistake"? He certainly knew how much you needed the recorder. Let's pray.'

So we bought the supplies and the bus tickets, we radioed to the pilot in Mitla to arrange a flight, and we left Mexico City. All the time we were very conscious that it was really our fellow Wycliffe members' money that we were now using. In Mitla we organised our cargo, sent a telegram to arrange for mules to meet us, and bought a basketful of fresh vegetables. The next morning we were up at the airstrip bright and early to weigh in. Too much weight, so what was essential? To live in Bill and Jay's house we had to take a full tank of calor gas for the gas stove, and we would have to carry on the medical work Bill had done, so the medicines had to go too. We would have another flight in about six weeks' time, so we cut tins, paper and personal supplies down to the minimum for that time. Still five lb. too much, so I took out potatoes (our morale booster), carrots and onions one by one and laid them on the scale like an offering. At four lb. the pilot reappeared on that sad scene to find Leslie feverishly re-tying boxes, and me by the scales.

'O.K., that'll do. We can take just one lb. extra, so let's load up. I don't know how long this good weather will last, as it's still the rainy season in your area.'

I gave the excess vegetables to his wife, and we were soon taxi-ing down the runway. It was quite a bumpy ride, with fluffy clouds on all sides; and as we crossed each of the four-mountain ranges on our route things ahead looked blacker. But the sun was still shining when we landed in Juquila, and it was thrilling to be back again, and to see the mules awaiting us. We unloaded quickly so that the plane would not get caught there by the weather, then turned our faces to the steep Yaitepec trail with anticipation — we really felt that we were coming home.

After a few months we found ourselves solvent again, and heaved a great sigh of relief, while thanking God again for that tape-recorder.

Leslie continued to work with Rodi or Lauro or his brother-in-law on the language, but it was a few hours here, and an hour or two there, which was not very satisfactory. So he started looking round for a regular language helper. Then he got to know an older blind man. Cinté had gone blind during a very severe illness in his early twenties, so he could remember seeing a great deal, but because of his blindness he could not make a cornfield. He was unmarried, and his relatives expected him to pay for all his food, etc., so he was always looking for some way to make a living. He jumped at the offer of regular work with Leslie, and proved to be a very good language helper. He was known as a good story-teller, so our new tape-recorder got lots of use. We learnt how the God of Thunder wears a different shirt according to the weather — a blue shirt on fine days, a black shirt for the rain, and a white shirt on the very windy days when gale-force winds blow tiles off people's roofs and bend the small trees nearly double. We learnt too how, once, the Chatinos had revolted against the Spanish speakers (at the end of the nineteenth century), and had come down from their mountain-top towns and villages and descended on the country town of Juquila in an angry mob massacring many people.

We had decided to make a detailed map of Yaitepec, marking every family compound and listing all the people in the family. Then we would pray for them household by household. This was easier said than done, as it took half-an-hour to walk from our house right up to the other side of the town, and there were numerous little side trails. Then there was the problem of names. No Chatino ever asks anyone: 'What is your name?', or asks a parent: 'What is your child's name?' The parent will give a false name for his child, and only under great duress will a person say his own name, and then often he does not give his real name. After you get to know people a little it is permissible to ask a third party 'What is his/her name?', but never the direct question. So we asked Cinté, but this meant explaining very carefully where the house was and who we were talking about, which greatly taxed our knowledge of the language.

Also as we went to visit sick people we were learning much more about the town and where people lived. However without formal medical training we found ourselves rather desperate sometimes, but we knew that God had put us there and we had to leave the results with Him. Then came a young nurse. Cynthia's church in Boston had sent her, and one or two others, down to Mexico as 'summer helpers' for six weeks or so. She gave us lots of useful tips and spent a great deal of time tramping over the mountainside from house to house with me, and giving advice on lots of cases.

July brings the fiesta of 'St. James-in-the-rain', when traditional horse-races are run on the only fairly level patch in the town, just outside the school. So Cynthia and I went to watch. The schoolmaster brought out chairs from his house for us to sit on, glad to have someone to talk to, even though our Spanish was very rudimentary. He and his wife spoke no Chatino, and most of the Yaitepec people spoke no Spanish, so he had a very hard time communicating with the children in his school, and it was a very lonely life for both him and his wife, with little social contact. However, on this day a number of young Spanish-speaking ranchers had come specially for the horse-racing. They were passing round tequila among themselves, and one or two were already rather tipsy, but they still insisted on racing, and we were expecting one to fall off at any minute. Then suddenly, one rather flushed, handsome young man mounted on a beautiful chestnut noticed Cynthia. Grabbing off his hat and sweeping her a deep bow he invited the Señorita to ride up in front of him and he would circle the course very sedately. She didn't understand and looked at me in bewilderment, so I told him that she didn't understand and could not ride anyway, thank you. He swept her another bow and brought the horse nearer. Then he said that he was sure that I, the Señora, would have no qualms if she rode with him since he was the best rider present and the most presentable escort. I was out of my depth now, knowing him to be a very rich and influential young man and lacking the necessary polite Spanish phrases to reply adequately. But the schoolmaster kindly and bravely came to our aid, apologising for our lack of Spanish and lack of knowledge of local customs, and asking him to please excuse the Señorita as she was unused to Mexican ways. The young man only laughed and replied: 'But she shall ride with me,' and started urging his horse towards our little group. Quick as a flash, the schoolmaster grabbed our arms and dragged us into his house while his wife undid the door that was tied open. She just banged it shut in time to stop the young man riding into the house after us. They quickly barricaded the door, and we could hear the horse being made to rear on the other side of it and scrape its hoofs on the door. I tried to apologise to the schoolmaster, hoping that the young man would not bear a grudge and use his family's influence against the teacher later for thwarting his desires like this. But the teacher replied:

'It is I who must apologise. I am ashamed to have such a pig for a fellow-countryman.'

Their little house was only about twelve feet by twelve feet, with a lot of space taken up by their double bed. Several other frightened women had fled inside along with us, so things were pretty crowded now, especially as we were keeping well away from the door which was still being battered, and obviously would not stand up to much more ill-treatment. Then we heard a friend call him away for another drink, and his attention was distracted. The teacher went into the little kitchen to reconnoitre through the cane walls of that rather temporary structure. A girl offered to lead Cynthia and I through the coffee bushes at the back and out to a roundabout trail home so, thanking the schoolteacher and his wife once again, we left.

Leslie had been taking pictures elsewhere, but he soon arrived home too.

'Cynthia, can you sew up a man's scalp? We only have an ordinary sewing needle and nylon cotton, but I'll sterilise that if you think it's any good. There is an injured Chatino man. He was drunk but insisted on racing and was thrown, and his horse's hind hoof caught the top of his head, so a great flap of hairy scalp is dangling. They have carried him home and I said we would follow.'

By the time we were ready the man's sister had arrived:

'Please come quickly. I'm sure he will die.'

Another patient arrived just then who had been cut by a matchet, so Leslie stayed to deal with him, and Cynthia and I went with the woman. The fog had rolled in and everywhere was damp and gloomy by this time, so that we could hardly see our way. The man's groans greeted us upon arrival, and he was obviously very drunk. He kept rolling backwards and forwards on his bed. I held the torch, and Cynthia gave him an injection, while water was being heated to wash out the mud from his head wound. I was amazed to see that it wasn't bleeding. Only by me sitting on him as I held the torch, and his sister holding his legs could we keep him still for Cynthia to wash out the wound and shave the scalp a little. The patient was quite oblivious to her ministrations, but did not like our restraint. Somehow she managed to get a few stitches in and tied, and some sort of dressing on. We bandaged his head pretty thoroughly and said we would be back the next day. Cynthia's only comment had been:

'If only a surgeon could see me now! All my careful training in sterile technique and hospital procedure! But it really didn't prepare me very well for a drunk on a foggy afternoon in a house with pole walls and an earth floor, and only a wobbly flashlight for light! Not to mention the sewing needle and thread, but at least that was sterile to start with!'

The wound healed well and there was no infection, but when we came to take the stitches out, our patient had gone with his mules on a contract as muleteer, so those little pieces of yellow nylon cotton stayed in . . .

One day not long after our return an old lady, previously unknown to us, came to ask Leslie to go and see her son. No, he could not walk down to our house. Yes, he was very ill with swelling and a high fever. Leslie went, complete with the medical book, and paper and pencil to send back a note if necessary. It turned out that the old lady and her son lived alone. He was about thirty but unmarried, and he certainly was very ill. It appeared to be mumps with extensive genital involvement, but there was no possibility of him going to hospital. Leslie gave him some aspirins and said:

'Look, these pills are just for the pain. I don't have any medicine to make him better, only God can do that. Let's talk to Him.' (This was the first time that Leslie had prayed in Chatino in public).

'All right,' said the old lady, and they knelt down in the middle of the earth floor. Leslie started to pray, and then paused, completely lost for words. We knew so little of the language at that point, and most of our knowledge was, of necessity, medical vocabulary. But as soon as he paused the old lady took it up and really prayed for her son's healing. By the time Leslie realised that she was now repeating the same words he had marshalled his thoughts, and when there was a slight pause he concluded the prayer and stood up. He was thrilled by the old lady's readiness to pray like that and then dumbfounded as she asked him:

'Which god did we talk to?'

He stumblingly tried to explain the truth to her, and then left saying he would be back the next day. At home we in turn prayed for help and wisdom and the man's healing. Leslie was anxious and went up there straightaway the next morning. He called the greeting as he approached the house, and the old lady came out to meet him with surprise.

'Did your son sleep last night? Is he a bit better today?'

'Oh yes. He's not here. He went out to work in the corn-field. The fever has gone, all the swelling has gone, and he is quite better.'

Leslie did not believe that he had heard correctly, and asked several more questions. We just had not expected that kind of instantaneous miracle. Then he said:

'Well, we asked God to heal him and He has, so let's go into your house and thank Him.'

It was the old lady's turn for amazement. The idea of thanking a deity was utterly foreign to her, but she com-plied, and Leslie came rushing home with the wonderful news. We praised our God and thanked Him too, and then we waited. We expected this wonderful news to spread like wildfire and people to come asking questions about the God of miracles, but no one came. So far as we know the old lady and her son never told anyone else what had happened, and they never wanted to know any more about it themselves. Why had God done that miracle? How had it brought glory to His Name? Finally we were forced to the humbling conclusion that He had done it for our benefit. He is dependable, He does supply what is necessary. He will make us able to do the job He has given us — it's not too big, we just need to be faithful. How much we had still to learn, and how much we have yet to learn! How gracious He is to bother to let us work with Him at all, but amazingly He wants our cooperation. There were other times when we were completely helpless and desperate, and we expected the Lord to do a miracle, but it was not the right time and He did not. Sometimes the patient died, and we grieved with the family knowing that not one of them knew or believed the One Who said, 'I am the Way, the Truth, and the Life.'

5

Whatever Will Happen Tomorrow?

WE NEVER KNEW what would happen from one day to the next. At Redcliffe, the unofficial motto had been: RFA (Ready for Anything), but as a student I had had no conception of what that 'anything' meant. It seemed as if we moved from one crisis to another, with hilarious incidents thrown in as punctuation. So often, the crises for the Chatinos were to do with illness and fighting, because the immediacy of death was a very fearful thing. On the other hand, they are tremendous jokers, with a well-developed sense of humour, and we never knew what significance an apparently ordinary event would have for them. Whenever there was a quiet lull and we could proceed with the ordinary routine of living and language work, the sense of impending crisis was always there. Cinté, our blind language helper, came every morning and was as good as a local newspaper in keeping us up-to-date with current events.

As we progressed in the language, and began to think about translation and literacy, we were very concerned about how to interest the people in learning to read. What would catch their interest? Particularly the women who only seemed interested in photos of people they knew. I had noticed that they were very accomplished needlewomen.

Several had sewing machines and they made their own very elaborate skirts (five yards of material for an everyday one, and seven yards for the ankle length four-tier one, worn on special occasions). They also made underskirts, the men's shirts (with special ruching down the front), and their pyjama-like calico trousers, as well as their own blouses. These blouses had elaborately embroidered yokes of intricate traditional design. Tema, the lady who had taught me to make tortillas, was an expert at this embroidery, and showed me her basket full of little pieces of cloth, with the different patterns embroidered on them. It suddenly occurred to me that perhaps a booklet of their own embroidery patterns, and a little writing, would lure them. So I made the first one, and it was very well received. We were encouraged, and prepared two more. We were concerned about the other Chatino villages and towns in the area, and felt that we ought to make contact with them too. So when the new embroidery leaflets arrived from our publications department in Mexico City, we began to plan a booklet-selling trip. Some time before, Bill and Jay had prepared a simple number booklet that the men seemed to enjoy, so we would take copies of that too.

Our opportunity came when we had two new members staying with us for tribal experience. One was a nurse, so we thought that they should be able to cope with any medical cases in our absence. They had been making quite an effort to study the language, and had shown a real interest in the people, but when we told them that for their last week they would be on their own, as we were going on this booklet-selling trip, they redoubled their efforts. So we packed up the booklets, a few medicines for emergencies, and a survival kit just in case, loaded up a hired donkey, and were off, following our guide. We decided to walk ourselves rather than ride this time, as we did not plan to go very far each day. We went to three different villages and stayed a night in each. They were very, very different, but we found a warm welcome in each place, and varying interest in the literature.

Each evening we visited the village 'agent' who, with a couple of assistants, was directly responsible to the nearest town council. These particular agents were all responsible to Juquila, the county town, and seemed pleased that we had come. We were also asked regularly if we had brought any medicine. We came home rejoicing in all the contacts made, and the number of booklets sold, and found the girls we had left behind in Yaitepec were rejoicing too. They confessed that they had never felt so despondent and utterly bereft as when they waved us off four days before. When their first visitors came, they felt like closing all the windows and barring the door, but instead they answered the greeting and then tried out some conversation. Early on they asked the question: 'Did you come for medicine?' If the answer was in the affirmative they had a special list of questions. The non-nurse did most of the talking. Then, she and the nurse conferred on what they thought were the symptoms. Their treatments seemed to have been successful, but they said that they had shared very fervent times of prayer together each evening, and they were delighted to see us back. In their spare time, they had creosoted a pile of new fence-posts for us that we needed badly. They had not wanted to be left alone there, but they felt that the experience was invaluable, and they had a heightened awareness of their trustworthy God as a result.

Cinté arrived for work one morning as usual, and as he sat down at the desk to start work with Leslie we heard a terrible wail:

'They've arrived now, that's his mother,' Cinté said.

'Whose mother? Who has arrived? What has happened?'

'Lauro's son was shot last night. The town messengers are carrying his body home now.'

'How? Why? Which son?'

'Rodi. He was found on the trail, and no one knows how it happened.'

The cry came again from across the gully, and I dashed out of the house and over to our former home. There was

Pescasia, quite overcome by grief, and I just took her in my arms while Granny opened the door of what had been our room, and motioned the bearers to carry in the body.

'I knew it would happen, I knew it. He knew it too, because he has been so afraid lately, but he would go out drinking with his friends. What shall I do, Kitty? I have only men-children, and they will all learn to shoot, and will all be killed. What is the good of all the pain to give birth, and all the work to feed them and bring them up, when they will just be shot, because I only seem able to produce men-children? But I'm better now. Don't worry about me. I must go and wash the body and put on his clean best clothes for the burial. No one but me can prepare the body.' We went in then, and after a little while I left her to it, as there was no further help I could give. At least it was not his father who had killed him. Later, the whole family fled from Yaitepec in fear of their lives — with good reason, since one by one Lauro and two more sons were all killed by different people.

We were deeply shocked by Rodi's death. We knew the family so well, it was like losing a relative. This debonair, intelligent, young man had had a special place in our hearts, and had helped Leslie a great deal with the language. Chatino is a tonal language, which means that the same word, said on a different pitch, usually has a completely different meaning. That is, it is really a different word. For instance, 'stone', flower', 'Mike' and 'head' are all spelt the same, but they are said on different pitches. In fact, the men can communicate just by whistling, without pronouncing any letters at all. Rodi had begun to teach Leslie this 'whistle-talk'. This was how warning of approaching danger (or anything else) was passed from house to house, and why no culprits were ever caught by outsiders in their home town. Now a real gap was left in our lives by the loss of this cheerful young man, and we grieved as we had not been able to introduce him to the Lord Jesus.

Life continued, and one day we became aware of four

little tomato plants in the garden. There was no running water, and no sink, in the house, but Bill had fixed up an ingenious drain for the dirty water with half an old biscuit tin inside the house, and tin cans soldered to it and to each other to make a pipe going out through the mud wall. There, curved tiles laid inside each other made a channel to take the water away from the house, and at the end of the channel were the four little tomato plants — they had seeded themselves from our dirty water. We quickly weeded round them, and began to look after them. They were about six to nine inches tall when we went off on a booklet-selling trip. On our return, only the smallest and least sturdy of the four was left. Then, passing our neighbour's house, we noticed three sturdy young tomato plants suddenly growing there, which we strongly suspected had not been there when we last passed by. We did not say anything, but we decided to tend our remaining plant very carefully, and see if we could not outdo the thief. It thrived and flourished. With delight we demonstrated its progress to our neighbours, and finally we picked ninety-six quite large tomatoes from it! We even gave some to those neighbours!

We were so pleased with the tomato results that we planted a little vegetable garden, and started a compost pit to help it along. We could always get bananas (we even had some plants in the garden) and other fruits when in season, but vegetables were a problem. Dried beans were available always, and certain varieties of squash, as well as a special variety of spring onion in its season, and horseradish, but not much else. The garden was a success and proved a good talking-point, but the interest was centred in seeing what kind of plants we foreigners grow to eat, not in trying out such vegetables for themselves. It was time for us to leave on another assignment for a few months, and, as the compost pit was full, we planned to bring back more seeds and have a bigger and better garden on our return.

In the middle of the rainy season we returned, and hacked our way from the gate to the porch through a jungle of undergrowth higher than our heads. In the process of clearing off the jungle in the days following, Leslie came upon various runners with leaves not unlike rhubarb leaves. Squash plants, but how? He followed them back to source, and found that they were all from one mighty plant rooted in the compost pit. We remembered that we had eaten some of the marrow-like chilacayote squash before leaving, and we must have thrown out some seeds with the rind on to the compost pit. The plant was certainly thriving on our compost, as the runners grew at least a foot a day. In fact, they took over the whole of the back garden, and they even climbed the guava and custard-apple trees, not to mention festooning the roof of our toilet — we did manage to keep the door free. We had noticed other people's chilacayote runners climbing trees, even the trees overhanging the main trail. As the fruit developed, somebody climbed up there and carefully protected each one with a rope bag — whether to protect the passer-by from an over-ripe chilacayote crashing on his head, or to protect their own property, I never quite knew.

Then we noticed that rather more people than usual were using the trail past our back fence, and inside the house we shamelessly listened in to their conversations.

'Look, they are growing chilacayote. They must have really settled down here.'

'Yes. What sort of harvest do you think they'll get?'

'Have to wait and see . . .'

It began to dawn on us that perhaps we had unwittingly done the Right Thing by Chatino standards. We listened some more.

'Look, they can really grow chilacayote.'

'Yes, do you think they would sell us one when they are ripe? How many plants do they have?'

'We could go in and ask . . .'

So began the visits and conducted tours to see the wonder-plant. We met people that we had never seen before, and we started a list of orders for the ripe fruit. Meanwhile we were eating the young ones daily, as they taste just like vegetable marrows when about the size of a four-ounce baby bottle. But it was a losing battle, and several were soon the size of full-grown marrows. Our visitors solemnly counted those big, striped, elongated balloon-like fruit, and exclaimed that there were nineteen on just one plant! We didn't dare divulge that we were eating up the young ones just as fast as we could, since obviously that could only be considered an anti-social action.

Our advisers told us that several of the fruit were just about ripe, so we consulted the list to see who to notify first. We would give away the extra ones to special friends, since it was plain that these chilacayotes were an acceptable gift. And then, the highest accolade of all. We counted the fruit once more, sixteen, seventeen ... where were the two dangling from the guava tree by the back fence? That's what comes of not taking note of the local way of doing things; doubtless they should have been protected by individual rope bags, we thought, as we rushed up to investigate. But there were no smashed remains under the tree. Then we looked up, and saw two neatly cut off stubs on the runners. They had been stolen, so somebody thought they were worth something. Our neighbours were highly indignant about the theft, and made wild speculations as to the culprits. (We had not told them about it, so we wondered how they knew of the theft at all . . .)

This decided us, and we set about the distribution of the fruit. We never dared tell our friends that we didn't eat a single one of the big, ripe ones, since we much preferred the tiny young ones. Nor did we say that we had not even planted the thing in the first place!

We never knew who would appear on our porch next, or for what reason. Our visitors were not only Yaitepec people, but sometimes came from other places. One morning we were surprised to hear an English greeting:

'Hullo there.'

We rushed to the door. Outside stood a tall American with a good camera and a very small pack. He had walked in from the coast road, finding his own trail! He identified himself as a free-lance writer for the *National Geographic* and other magazines. We invited him in, and he stayed for several days, but he insisted on paying his way. He was most interested in the Chatino people, but was very tactful about taking photos, not wishing to break the local conventions. He also joined in with our times of family prayers, and was quite willing to *discuss* the Gospel, but insisted that nobody could be a businessman and a Christian at the same time. One morning he left, still on foot, and we have heard no more of him.

Another time, a messenger arrived from Juquila, with a note from our Spanish-speaking friend there:

> Please excuse the intrusion and the interference, but could you possibly help the authorities down here? An English-speaking pilot crashed his plane while landing on the airstrip here this morning, and he speaks no Spanish. He is unhurt, and we have notified the aviation inspector in Oaxaca City by telegram. Could you do us the favour of coming down to interpret, please?

Leslie went off with the messenger saying, 'I'll probably bring him back with me to stay with us meantime, since he can't communicate with anyone down there.'

In the afternoon, I saw them coming and made a cup of tea. Although this pilot had been flying small planes for some time, he had never flown in the mountains, nor had he attempted to land on a one-way airstrip before, with the side of a mountain along one side and a precipice on the other. He had badly dented one wing by running into the mountainside to stop himself. Also, he had never flown outside the U.S.A., and seemed quite ignorant of international aviation conventions. He just wanted to come to Juquila, so he got into his plane and flew down.

'But why Juquila? It hardly even appears on the map.'

'My wife is very ill. I've taken her to all the clinics and

specialists, and they can do nothing, they say. I have tried various other cures and ways of healing, and nothing has helped yet. I am willing to try anything, and money is no object. Then I heard about the sacred narcotic mushroom. I know that lots of people have gone to Huautla in the Maxatec area, but it seems to be very commercial there, with tourists and drop-outs just going for the experience of eating the mushroom. Then I heard about the curer here in Juquila who uses the mushroom for healing, so I came to find out about it. I guess I didn't realise that it would be quite so hard to communicate, but you can speak their lingo. Will you take me to this curer fellow and see if the patient has to be here, or perhaps he could perform the ceremony long-range like, if I buy some mushrooms to take back for her to eat? I'll pay him well, and if he needs to come to her, I'll see about that too.'

We knew about the mushroom and its narcotic effects. We also knew that it had been investigated medically, and it did not have the magical healing properties that were claimed for it. We knew too that it was illegal to take plants of any sort across the U.S.A. border without a special permit, and we saw how desperate this man was. We tried to explain all this, tactfully and sympathetically, and we tried to point him to the Scriptures.

'God helps those who help themselves. I know that. I've got the money, and I expect to pay for her healing, but how can God help me if I don't take some responsibility myself and explore every possibility of help for her that I know of?

A day or so later, another messenger from Juquila arrived. The note said that the inspector had arrived, and could Leslie please bring the man down and interpret, as everything was highly irregular, and the pilot would probably have to face legal charges. They went. It turned out that the pilot had not officially filed his flight plans, or had them approved by the authorities. The plane was impounded, and he was to accompany the inspector back to Oaxaca City to find an English-speaking lawyer to keep him out of jail.

No one knew if he would ever get legal permission to return to Juquila himself to consult the curer or get hold of the mushrooms.

Then there was the Spanish-speaking lady from Juquila, with her twenty-year-old son. He looked rather pale but otherwise fairly fit, although, obviously, the thousand-feet climb up from Juquila on foot had tired him a bit. His mother said that they had had to stop to rest many times, and that he had not been able to work for several years. He had the 'illness of fear', she said. It all began when he fell into a pool and was almost drowned as a boy, and his parents had taken him to all the curers in Juquila. He had eaten the narcotic mushroom several times, and done all the other things they told him to do, but all to no avail. They had even taken him to the doctor in Oaxaca City, and he had faithfully endured the injections and taken all the medicine, but it was no good. Was there anything we could do? Obviously, there was nothing more that we could do medically, but we asked all the check-up questions just in case. Then Leslie talked to them about the Lord Jesus. We had copies of the Gospel in 'popular' Spanish, and Leslie asked him to read out loud whole passages concerning forgiveness of sins and the healing of the sick. They also read of the crucifixion and the resurrection, and the young man and his mother listened eagerly. The young man just lapped it up and almost forgot his own physical state in his excitement over the wonderful Gospel message. He saw the application to himself, and he wanted to pray. He asked for God's forgiveness and he asked the Lord to take over his life, and then he asked too for healing. They stayed several hours, and were delighted to be able to buy those Gospels. As they left, Leslie gave him some salt pills.

'Look, you are going to start working again now, and your body isn't used to it, so when the sun's heat makes you feel a bit giddy or faint, just take one of these with a glass of water. These are not a cure, just a help when you are working.'

People often said that they (or especially their children)

were suffering from the 'sickness of fear', but usually there were definite medical symptoms that responded to the appropriate medicine; they were just blaming some unfortunate accident in the past — like falling into water — for quite recent symptoms that they didn't understand. However, that had not been the case with this young man, and we praised God for the fellow's eagerness to hear and accept the Truth. We trusted that he had truly joined God's family, but we wondered how he would go on.

About a fortnight later, he came again. We hardly recognised the healthy-looking, smiling but shy, young man with the springy step, who proudly introduced us to his father. This man was one of the skilled matchet-makers in Juquila. After chatting for a little, and saying happily how delighted they were at the change in their son, he produced a presentation matchet engraved with patterns all over the blade and the legend 'Recuerdo de Juquila' (in remembrance of Juquila) on it. He and his son had made it specially for Leslie, to show their friendship and gratitude. The young man told us that yes, he was still reading the Scriptures that he had bought, but surely there was more? We gave him the address of the Bible Society in Mexico City, and told him that they would help him get in touch with the nearest group of Christians. That was a really thrilling day.

Leslie came in from a medical call one day, and sat down heavily on a chair, tired and discouraged.

'I don't know where to start with this fellow, Nino, he has so many things wrong with him, and yet so much of his serious condition now is from sheer neglect, I'm sure. He's an orphan, so when his wife felt that she could not look after him any longer, they carried him down to his ancient grandparents' house to die, while she took the children with her to her own parents' place. It was his granny that fetched me this morning, just in case I could do something. With every new symptom they restricted his diet even more, out of fear, so that now he subsists on dry tortillas and salt only, with a small amount of warm water to drink. I'm going to ask the doctor on the radio — there is no reason for Nino to die from neglect and starvation.'

Leslie then wrote a list of all Nino's symptoms in Spanish, to make sure that he included everything that he could, and dictated the list over the radio to the pilot. In the afternoon the pilot had one or two further check questions to ask, and the next day he read out the prescription. We did not have all the necessary medicines on hand, so the pilot said he would get them and send them, together with the prescription and a covering note from the doctor, by post. Meanwhile Leslie could start with some that we did have.

He visited Nino every day, and it soon became plain that he would not make fast progress so long as he stayed in that house, because his grandmother was too bound by custom and traditional beliefs to feed him properly. However, everyone was very impressed when he evacuated a huge quantity of intestinal worms and started complaining that he was hungry. After about a week, the medicine arrived with the doctor's letter.

'Look, it means giving medicine after a small meal seven times a day! They will never do that at his house,' said Leslie. 'Would you be willing to have him here for the duration? That's ten days or so. It will mean lots of extra work for you, but at least we could control the situation then, and probably save his life.'

'Can he walk at all?' I asked.

'Yes, with help, and I'll see to that. We can get Grandad to cut him a stick, anyway.'

'Well, let's get him down here and start as soon as possible, then. What about the cost?'

'I thought we could just charge them an all-in subsidised figure, and not tell them how much each medicine costs, because Nino himself has nothing, after being ill so long, and the grandparents have paid out thousands of pesos to witch-doctors and curers already. I'll go and talk to them now, and you will have to work out some simple menus that fit the doctor's recommendations here in his letter.'

Nino arrived the next day, slumped on the back of a mule that his grandfather was leading, and he just managed to totter into the house. We soon had him tucked up in bed and started his hospital regimen. Granny had sent a rope-bag full of dried tortillas with him so that he would not starve. So the first thing was to take these away, as the doctor had said, '*No* corn at all for the first few days, just a very bland diet.'

We began with thin soup with a few noodles in it.

'I'm not going to eat those worms. I'm not an animal,' was Nino's reaction. We showed him the dry noodles. We explained what they were made of, and we told him what the doctor had said.

'I'll just die without tortillas,' he said.

'Look, you are already a bit better because of the medicine you have taken. You came here to our house because you said you wanted to have all the medicine that the doctor had ordered. You must trust us a little more, and eat the food that the doctor ordered too. Anyway, it's very bad manners to call the food that Kitty cooked specially for you, "those worms". Of course she wouldn't feed you worms — whoever heard of people eating worms?'

So, with great suspicion, he ate the soup and 'worms' and took his first dose of medicine. He progressed through jelly, milk puddings, cream soups, strained vegetable, egg custards, fish and rice, to meat and mashed beans, etc. On the fifth day, he had a small piece of tortilla with each savoury dish, and things really began looking up. He started to walk outside a little, even without his stick. At first he lost weight alarmingly, but he was getting rid of all the excess fluid that had caused his bloated, unnatural, oedematous shape. Then he began putting on weight with firm flesh where he had just been skin, water and bone before. At the end of the treatment, he walked home all the way up the hill, to the amazement of his grandparents. He continued taking strengthening medicine — like vitamins — for some time, but he was better. A mixture of parasites taking over his body had been the cause of his illness, through ignorance and lack of care, and now they were gone, but obviously he could do with some good food for several months.

We had been asked to go to a linguistic 'workshop' — a study conference where we would get expert advice to help us sort out the tone patterns and the grammar of the language. We would also be able to concentrate on the desk work, without the interruptions of life in Yaitepec, and it would be good to talk things over with fellow workers from other related languages. There was just one snag. Who would go with us as a language helper? We wondered if we could combine Nino's need of convalescence with our need of a Chatino companion for this venture. Leslie went to talk to the family, and so it was arranged. We learnt a great deal about how the Chatino language works during that workshop, and Nino learnt a little bit about the Lord Jesus Christ, and grew healthy and strong physically. When he returned home, his wife and children returned to him, and he was able to work and support them all.

Back in Yaitepec, Cinté came regularly again, and, having sorted out some of the linguistic problems, Leslie now began his first attempt at translation. Old Cinté was fascinated as they worked their way through Mark's Gospel together, and he asked all sorts of questions. It was a tremendous thrill for us to have got to the translation stage at last, especially as Cinté seemed so eager to learn it all. They finished that first rough draft, and then we went on furlough to England.

The Lord had been at work, and while we were away, the Upson family was able to return to Mexico with a fairly clean bill of health. Nino and his family went with them to a translation workshop where that Gospel of Mark was revised, checked, re-checked and improved, and finally made ready for the printer. So at last Nino and his family were able to understand what the Gospel message was all about.

PART TWO

At Home in a Coconut Grove

6

A New Assignment

WE RETURNED FROM furlough, and came back to the original question again — where does God really want us? We went to see our Director and found that he had been considering this too.

'I wonder if it isn't time we started thinking about the third Chatino area now Bill and Jay are back and can cover the Yaitepec section. According to your survey report, Leslie, you got a great welcome from the people there, but we've never taken them up on it.'

'Well, it is the smallest Chatino group. There are only about 2,000 speakers of that language, which is why we felt so sure that we should go to Zenzontepec first.'

'Yes, but the Zenzontepec door closed, and still seems to be closed, so I think that you should investigate the situation in and around Tataltepec. Let's pray.'

This was a bombshell, but, all right, we would go and investigate. We were prepared to start again, but not very convinced that God really required this of us. Back to the old routine! We bought some basic supplies and equipment, packed and shipped them, then caught the overnight coach to Oaxaca City, and so to Mitla. It was a warm, encouraging feeling to meet old friends there at the centre, and to know their fellowship in this new venture. We knew that there was an airstrip at Tataltepec, but we didn't know how often it was used, or what condition it was likely to be in now that the rains were about to begin. We decided to pack up two months' supplies plus our other things, and leave them ready in the hangar at the M.A.F. centre, hopeful of later transport. Leslie made some packing-case cupboards, just the right size to load on one side of a mule, and he painted them bright green as a morale booster, in anticipation of our new home. Then we studied the map and decided on our route.

We knew that Tataltepec was twelve hours' walk from Juquila, but it seemed to be only about eight hours from Jamiltepec, and a second-class bus from Oaxaca City could take us all the way to Jamiltepec. We found out that the bus left Oaxaca at seven a.m., so we packed a few belongings in a kit-bag, stuffed one of the new green cupboards full of emergency medicines and basic foods, packed a picnic bag, and went to Oaxaca City for the night. Six forty-five a.m. saw us at the bus station, pushing through the crowd towards the Pacific coast bus. The conductor was up on the roof receiving boxes and bags of various shapes and sizes, so Leslie passed ours up too, while I got inside to find a seat. By seven a.m. the bus was crowded to capacity, and we could hear somebody's chicken squawking from the bus roof. The driver got in, and we started off with the jostling crowd parting to let the bus through to the gate.

It was a bright, sunny day, and by the time we stopped for breakfast at nine a.m., it was blazing hot and we were sticking to our seats. The driver and some passengers filed into the little road-side café, while local vendors plied their wares at the bus windows — fresh orange juice; slices of pineapple or watermelon; *tamales* (meat pasties, with maize dough for the pastry, wrapped individually in banana leaves or corn husks); bottled soft drinks; chewing gum, and so on. Like several other passengers, we just bought bottled drinks, and dug into our picnic bag.

After breakfast we began to climb steadily into the high mountains of the Mixteca Alta region of the Sierra Pacifica. The rains had begun here, and it started to get quite cold and foggy, so we stopped again for the driver and conductor to fix a big tarpaulin over the cargo (and the chicken).

It was still quite foggy, and trying to rain, as we careered down a mountainside in the afternoon. We roared round a corner, and then came to a screeching halt as the driver applied the brakes with a jerk. The road ahead was blocked by a land-slide — no doubt the earth had been loosened by the rain. The driver and conductor got out, but there was nothing that they could do of course, except wait. There were no settlements or houses close by, and people began speculating as to whether we would have to spend the night there. Nearly everyone got out to stretch their legs and to examine the bit of mountainside that had fallen in our way. We could see the road going on down the mountainside beyond the land-slide, and we wondered what other vehicles would join us to wait on that lonely stretch of road.

Even though it was the end of May, it began to get dark early because of the fog and drizzle. Then we heard something coming up the mountainside beyond the land-slide. It crawled into sight, and we could see that it was a road works machine of some kind. It turned out to be a bulldozer, and in a very short while it had bulldozed that impassable pile of earth off the road and over the precipice into the valley below. We quickly settled ourselves back in the bus, and off we went again.

At midnight we arrived in Pinotepa Nacional, and were told that the bus would leave again at six a.m. sharp. We had not known of this 'night stop' and, because of the delay at the land-slide, the bus had arrived in the town much later than usual. Several passengers shook out rugs or shawls, arranged themselves on the pavement by the bus stop with their belongings, and settled down to sleep if they could. We were just debating whether to get out our sleeping bags and do the same, when a young man appeared and said to us in particular, and to the passengers in general: 'Do you want the hotel or the *posada*? I will show you the way.'

As there weren't many hours left till six a.m., and we

knew that the hotel would be more expensive, we settled for the *posada* — a place that just gives overnight accommodation. Two or three other passengers went with us. Our guide woke up the proprietor when we got to the *posada*, and told him of our needs. There was a covered walk surrounding a big courtyard and the rooms led off this. They had concrete floors and were simply furnished with camp beds. The communal toilet facilities were at one corner of the courtyard.

All too soon it was time to get up and go back to the bus. We passed a hotel and a few other rather imposing buildings as we started off, and an hour later we had climbed up into the foothills to the town of Jamiltepec. This little Mixtec town was the end of the road for us, so we gathered our belongings together, left the bus, and went into the market to get some breakfast.

The Spanish-speaking friend in Juquila who had been such a help to all our predecessors in Yaitepec, and who had taken us to his large heart too, had a grand-daughter living in Jamiltepec. Her husband had a most responsible federal government office in the town and district, and our Juquila friend had given us a letter of introduction to him, so now we went over to the Town Hall to find his office. He received us very cordially, suggested a widow who would be willing to accommodate us in Jamiltepec, and sent a town messenger over to advise her of our coming. Then he discussed the route to Tataltepec, and the need for mules and a guide. We would have to cross the Rio Verde by canoe at El Paso de la Reina (Queen's Pass, or El Paso for short), so he wrote a further note of introduction to the agent there, urging him to help us. He said that he would let us know when he had found the necessary mules, and invited us up to his house to see his wife that evening. Then a town messenger took us to the widow's house where we were glad to rest.

The matter of the mules and the guide was arranged, and we took leave of our new friend that same day, as we were to start off early the next morning. We filled our water bottles with boiled water, knowing that it would be hot on the open trail once we got outside Jamiltepec. This place was like an oasis with its grove of coconut palms and mango trees, and the beautiful bushes of hibiscus and bougainvillea. We got off to a good start in the morning. Our guide was very familiar with the trail, and he stopped hopefully at every water hole; but the rains were overdue, and everything was dried up. We stopped for a meal at a little village, and got a drink there, but then came a long, dry, barren stretch, and we gave him our third water bottle. We found that we had over-estimated our stamina, and under-estimated the heat. So, for the last mile or two to El Paso, the guide led my mule, and I just sat slumped in the saddle, hanging on to the pommel, semi-conscious from dehydration.

The guide took us straight to the agent's house in El Paso, where we were made very welcome by the agent's wife in his absence. She brought us water to drink and made me lie down on her own bed, while Leslie rested in their hammock. The blissful shade of the house, with its watered earth floor to make it cooler, helped a lot. After a little rest and several pints of water, I felt a bit better but clearly, it was not sensible to attempt the last three hours of the journey that day. The woman had sent a child off to the field to take the letter of introduction to her husband, and he soon arrived, with profuse apologies that he had not been on hand to welcome us. In time he got round to asking us why we were going to Tataltepec. He was quite intrigued by the idea of writing down the hitherto unwritten Tataltepec Chatino language, and then making books. This was obviously a brand new idea to him, but he could see the value of it — particularly the value of a bilingual dictionary with Chatino and Spanish — although he was not quite so convinced of the need for Chatino Scripture.

In the evening he went out to arrange for mules, a guide and the canoe crossing, ready for the next morning. He insisted that we stay with them for the night, and use his bed, while he and his wife slept on a mat on the earth floor of the kitchen. They entertained us royally, and seemed sorry to say goodbye in the morning.

The agent himself came with us to the river bank, where another man was waiting with the broad dugout canoe. The river was quite flooded from the rains which had fallen up in the mountains. Rio Verde means 'Green River', but the muddy red-brown torrent was certainly not living up to its name that day. It had risen several feet, they said, and the current was strong, but, since no trees or large logs were being carried past, they felt it was safe to attempt the crossing.

We got in, and crouched down on the bottom of the canoe with the baggage and the saddles, along with the guide. There were just two paddles, so the agent and the canoe-man took these, one at each end of the canoe. Then the mules were pulled into the water upstream from the canoe and we started out. As we got out into the river the current was very strong, and we seemed to be rushing downstream at an alarming rate, but as I glanced back at the shore, I saw that we really were making headway as well. I had wondered why the canoe was dragged so far upstream before we started out, and now I realised that every yard of that anticipated drift would be used, as we would arrive on the other side several hundreds of yards further downstream. The mules were battling along beside us, but the current gradually forced them right up against the upstream side of the canoe. Then they started to be dragged underneath, so the agent yelled to us to keep the animals' heads above the surface so that they would not drown. This all made the work of paddling much harder, but at last we broke out of the current, and into the slack water on the other side, from where they paddled easily back upstream to the landing place. The mules struggled up the bank gratefully and stood trembling. We got out of the canoe no less gratefully. After wiping the animals down a bit, the agent and the guide re-saddled them and loaded up the cargo. Then we said goodbye to that energetic and helpful man, the agent, and they paddled upstream for some distance before waving as they turned out into the mainstream again for the crossing.

The guide said that he was very surprised that we had been able to cross that morning, and that the canoe-man would never have attempted it if the agent had not been there. We thanked God again for His help and protection as we started off up the steep side of the river gorge. The red clay was very slippery from the rain, and the smaller rocks all seemed ready to roll from under the mules' hooves, but finally we came out over the rim. With a last glance at the dirty river far below us now, we moved on along the trail through beautiful rolling countryside, grateful for the shade of the big mango and wild fig trees in the dried up stream beds and gullies. Then we topped a rise, and our guide pointed to a distant, hazy grove of coconut palms.

'That's Tataltepec,' he said.

We were riding down into a bowl with bumps on the bottom and mountains towering up in a semi-circle. Soon we came to a gate across the trail, and a barbed wire fence stretched away on either side. This was to keep the cattle out of the irrigated fields and gardens immediately outside the town, our guide told us.

'Is there a gate like this on every trail then?'

'Yes, and it is a punishable offence to leave it open behind you.'

We passed through and closed it. Then, round the next bend, we met a cavalcade leaving the town. Sergio, the youngest son of our Spanish-speaking friend in Juquila, and his wife, María, had told us that if we ever visited Tataltepec, we should go straight to María's mother, Doña Emelia, and she would look after us. Sergio and María had obviously passed on the word, because one of the ladies of the party immediately recognised us and introduced herself as Sergio's mother-in-law, before we could speak. She seemed very glad to see us, and apologised profusely that it was necessary for her to make this trip for a few days now, so that she could not welcome us properly to her home.

'My eldest son and my daughter Catalina are at home. Tell them that you saw me, and that you are to stay with us. My son here is just escorting me to the river crossing, so he will be back tonight too. I will be back in a few days and we will talk then.'

Doña Emelia told our guide to take us straight to her shop, and to tell Catalina who we were. He did so without bothering to consult us, and we soon realised that whatever Doña Emelia said was respected throughout the area. Our stock had definitely gone up in our guide's eyes when he realised that we were to be taken under Doña Emelia's wing.

Catalina was just as charming, and in her mother's absence was the perfect hostess. She rushed forward with seats when we came into the shop, and ran to get bottled soft drinks to serve us. As we knew that the bottles of drink had to come on the backs of pack animals by the same route that we had come, we marvelled again at the generosity of these people. We were glad to relax for a few minutes in the coolness of the store, and we glanced round at the shelves as we chatted with Catalina. Bales of multi-coloured material of varying qualities (including one of fine lace, to my surprise), unbleached calico, cotton blankets, embroidery silks and cottons of every hue, notebooks, pencils, rubbers, crayons, ball-pens, torches, batteries, sandals, shirts, trousers, hats, underclothes, rope, buckets, oil lamps, matchets, bullets, nails, tins of sardines, matches, aspirins, cod liver oil, milk of magnesia, Vick Vapour Rub and a few other patent medicines, tins of powdered milk, packets of cornflour, tins of chile peppers, onions, rice, dried beans, chiles, pottery and enamel cups and dishes, cigarettes, and many other things were to be seen; while on the floor were open sacks of flour, sugar and maize, and in jars on the counter were sweets, biscuits and noodles. It was definitely a 'general store', not unlike the village shop at home.

Leslie went out to see the guide off on his return journey, and then Catalina took us round to another little house next door. She showed us a bed, and told us that this was the 'young men's room'. We later discovered that this meant her two older brothers and another young man who lived with them.

During all of this, we had seen inquisitive children peeping round corners at us, but all keeping their distance. As we had come into the town we had seen several people slip into their houses, and we knew we had been watched through the pole walls as we passed. It was strange to ride into a Chatino place and not to hear greetings sung out from all sides. People we met on the trail greeted us in Spanish, and hurried on, but no one called out from their houses. The town too was very different from Yaitepec. Here there were coconut palms, mango trees, and other leafy trees providing shade, as well as the plum and tamarind trees. But there were none of the hedges or fences that we were used to, no green bushes and grass—just small houses crowded together, made with pole walls and with bare, dusty earth between them, where the pigs and chicken roamed about at will. There were a few of the bigger, adobe mud-brick houses to which we were accustomed, but it soon became apparent that most of these belonged to the richer Spanish-speakers, such as the shop-keepers.

After stowing our belongings under our bed, we thought we should go and report to the Town Hall. We needed to explain our presence to the authorities, and to ask their permission to investigate the linguistic situation in their area. Some men remembered Leslie's visit with Bill four years before, and they were very glad to see him again now. They wanted to know if we were going to settle in their town, and if we had brought any medicine. Leslie assured them that yes, we had brought a little medicine, and that more would come later when we had found out where it was best to live. Then he enquired about the villages round about. They readily gave him a list, and explained that all were inhabited by entirely Spanish-speaking people, except El Paso, where we had crossed the Rio Verde. A number of Chatino families from Tataltepec had moved down there, but all the rest of the speakers of the Tataltepec Chatino language lived right here in this one town. Then they offered a town messenger on duty as guide to show us round the town, and to introduce us to some of the people, so that we could start learning the language. That was how we first met Juvencio.

He was a small, thin man, with bright, flashing eyes. He was grasping his official stick to show that he was on duty, and was wearing the usual white pyjama-like trousers with the cross-over front, and strings to tie at the back. They were made of unbleached calico, and his coloured shirt had been made locally too. He wore a black felt hat, and spoke to us slowly in Chatino. We followed him along a trail leading away from the square, and up to the first house. He greeted the people, and they invited us all in. Then he explained who we were, and that we had lived in Yaitepec before, but now we wanted to learn the 'real Chatino', so we had come here, and we would be writing it down on paper. They promptly told us a word or two, which we obediently repeated and wrote down. Then the paper was passed round and exclaimed over, and when it got back to us, we read out the words again. They were amazed and delighted. We moved on to the next house, and the procedure was repeated. By the third house we were able to mimic the initial greeting, and to get that written down too. We had already realised that greetings to people that we met on the trail, and greetings to people in their homes, were different, just as in Yaitepec Chatino. We had also found that the Yaitepec Chatino greetings did not help us very much in this town.

At the third house, we found an elderly, but very sprightly, granny at home alone. After a few minutes, Leslie and Juvencio left to continue their tour, and I chose to remain and see how I got on. We were still quite close to the Town Hall, so I could easily get back to Doña Emelia's house. The old lady seemed glad that I stayed, and became a firm friend. She was very patient with me, and so pleased when I wrote down her words. I went back to see her two or three times in the succeeding days.

Later, we excitedly compared notes. We felt that it had been a very profitable first day, but now there was the matter of meals. We could not just continue to sponge on Catalina; there must be someone in the town who cooked meals for travellers. Catalina sent a younger brother to guide us to the house of an aunt who was known to be a good cook. We were greeted warmly, and once again we had the feeling of having been expected. We discussed this after supper as we strolled back to our sleeping quarters: first, Doña Emelia on the trail had not been a bit surprised to see us, just pleased that we had come; Catalina too seemed to have been forewarned; then the authorities at the Town Hall — how had they known that we might help them medically? Why did they think we would want to settle here permanently and learn the language? They seemed to take it as a challenge to convert us from the barbaric, uncouth mountain speech of Yaitepec to the 'pure' Chatino of Tataltepec as fast as possible. Now the lady providing meals seemed all prepared.

We had expected to live in a little village away from the main town, but as we asked one and another, we found that everyone gave the same answer as the authorities; other than Tataltepec itself, the only place where there were speakers of this Chatino language was El Paso, where they were the minority. Perhaps this town was the right place to stay — it certainly seemed to be prepared for our coming.

Leslie decided to go back to the Town Hall and ask if there were any houses to rent in the town if we decided to stay, and what they would expect of us. Also, what sort of condition the airstrip was in, and if we would be able to use it. This time he met the town president, who was a Spanish-speaker. He was no less welcoming than his Chatino colleagues. He was sure that there would be a house available, and he thought there was an empty one almost next door to where we went for meals. We should enquire there.

This house turned out to be right next door to the president himself, and it belonged to his brother, who lived with his one family in a little village down near the Rio Verde, but came into town to stay with his other family for the weekends. Everyone was quite sure that the owner wanted to lease us the house, and urged us to take up residence in the kitchen meanwhile — it was unlocked — and the owner would bring the key of the big main house at the weekend. Again, it all seemed pre-arranged, and we were becoming more and more convinced that our Master the real Director had been here first and prepared the way. We had come here expecting to investigate and to pioneer for a week or two, and yet we found ourselves with the answers to all our main questions after only three days. We seemed to have been following a carefully planned scheme ever since we got off the bus in Jamiltepec, and we had been very aware of God's presence with us in these days. We had prayed and done some Bible study together, and we had been reminded of several passages that speak of God's guidance and planning for people. So now we moved into this kitchen, bought a load of firewood and set up housekeeping.

Then the visitors started to come. Catalina sent one of her younger brothers or sisters almost daily with some little present of fresh mangos, eggs, tomatoes or something. Not to be outdone, the president's family sent over the younger boys with other presents of food, while the lady who had provided us with meals sent us some fresh, new, sweet bread rolls. Someone gave us some cooking bananas, so I baked some banana bread, and then we were able to return the courtesy visits of these new friends and neighbours.

At the weekend, the president's brother turned up with the key. He seemed very glad to see us and quite agreeable to letting his house to us. We were to pay the rent fortnightly. He took us in to view it, and said he would let it to us as it stood, furnished. There were four chairs, three tables, and a bed. There was one good-sized window at the back, of the usual wooden shutter type, a brick floor, and two big, double doors at the front leading on to a wide verandah-type porch, with a low wall round it, which ran the whole length of the house. The house had very thick, adobe mud-brick walls plastered white, and was one enormous long room inside. Steps led up to the porch as the house was built on a slope.

We slept in our new home that night.

7

Early Days

As soon as we moved into that big main house, the numbers of visitors stepped up — people seemed to feel that now we were a permanency. The president himself drifted over to our porch in the evenings, or called Leslie over to his own beautifully shady porch with its trained flowering vine trailing along it as a living screen. He took a fatherly interest in us, and kept a close check that we were in good health, knew where to get all that we needed, and that we were not being imposed upon or cheated by anyone.

Now that we had a house to put them in, we began to feel the need of our goods and chattels. Cooking on an open wood fire is a challenge and can be fun, but it is not a very efficient use of time when you have a little table-top gas stove all packed up and waiting for you. Also, eating out of mess tins and spare tin cans is convenient, but it has its limitations. People were beginning to ask for medical help too, so we needed the medicines that we had left behind. But, most of all, we needed our books and language materials, and the other things that we had left up in Yaitepec. So we told the president that we needed to go back up to Yaitepec for a week, to close up the house there, say goodbye to our friends, and collect our belongings. Juvencio's brother, José, was to come with us as guide, and to bring the mules back.

'We will come back in the little plane a week from today,' Leslie told the president as he waved us off early in the morning.

The rains had started the week before, and so everything was fresh and green as soon as we got to the edge of the town. We climbed up over Bean Mountain, and came to the village of Tepenixtlahuaca — the farthest outpost of the mountain Chatino language. People looked out of their houses, and the familiar mountain greetings were sung out. Without thinking, we easily dropped back into the mountain speech that we were trying to change for the sake of the people of Tataltepec. We found a house where they would serve us breakfast, and gratefully slid off our mules. José was amazed, after our stumbling efforts with his language, to hear us amicably chatting and joking with the people here, and to hear them asking us for medicine.

The path got muddier as we went on, and the atmosphere cooled off as we climbed higher up the valley with each little ridge. The mud slowed down our progress, and after dinner in Panixtlahuaca with the same friendly reception, we saw the blue-black, heavy rainclouds piling up above us. They threateningly seemed ready to squash us, and then, with a searing flash of lightning and an ear-splitting crack, the cloud-taps turned full on. Even with rain-capes, we were soaked in a few minutes, and muddy water streamed down the mountainside to meet us — the trail made a good river bed. The mules put their heads down and plodded on, sometimes up to their knees in mud and water. For a little while the noise was deafening as the water rushed down the trail, and the rain battered the trees and branches of the forest around us. We thought of the town messengers who made this trip to Juquila twice weekly, rain or shine, to collect the Tataltepec mail from the post office there. On foot, travelling light, and knowing all the short cuts, it usually took them between eight and ten hours one way.

The rain stopped and we made better time. It was still misty and getting late now, so the light was very poor as we topped the last ridge and looked down towards Juquila. The mist cleared and the moon came out as we reached the river ford at the edge of the town. It was quite cold now, and the small river had swollen with the rain, so that the mules had trouble getting across loaded with us, but they kept their footing, and our bedraggled little party wended its way to the house of our good Spanish-speaking friend. We turned into his yard just twelve hours after leaving Tataltepec. His ferocious watch-dog announced our arrival, and Don Alfonso himself appeared smiling his welcome. Our clothes had almost dried on us, so we felt more comfortable now, although poor José was shivering from the cold of the unaccustomed altitude. Don Alfonso showed him where to get feed for the mules, and then showed us a room next to his own. He plied us with questions about Tataltepec. He wanted to know about our reception and how his daughter-in-law's family had treated us. He did not want us to leave the immediate vicinity, but he was sure that they really needed our help down in Tataltepec; 'Especially medical help,' he said.

Next morning we climbed up to Yaitepec. Our approach had been noticed, and the friendly greetings warmed our hearts. From long experience of our comings and goings, one of the first questions was:

'How long are you staying?'

They were rather dismayed when we said, 'Just for a week,' and that we had moved to Tataltepec.

'But you can't learn Chatino down there! We don't understand a word they say, and we hardly know that they *are* real Chatino people. This is the only place to learn the real, "standard" Chatino speech.'

We assured them that Bill and Jay would be back again, and that Yaitepec was not forgotten.

The week passed quickly as we visited all our friends, and packed everything into mule-loads, then weighed it all and marked it for the plane flight. For the last time, we closed the door of that house in Yaitepec, and put the padlock on it.

We closed the gate behind us and wired it up. Then we followed the mules down to the airstrip to meet the plane. The pilot came with the cargo we had left in the hangar, and filled up the flight with one of us, while the other stayed with the rest of the baggage. He then made shuttle flights down the valley to Tataltepec.

A tremendous crowd turned out to see the plane. As we circled over the strip we could see men, women and children running along the trails from their homes to the landing field. Then we were down, and people surged in from all sides to engulf the plane. The president's family and Doña Emelia received us back with the customary Mexican hug, and town messengers had been sent from the Town Hall to carry our luggage. With both of us on the ground again, and our belongings piled up round us, the pilot said a hasty goodbye, and that he would be listening for us. He wanted to beat the afternoon rain, and we could already see the ominous, fat blackness menacingly bearing down upon us from the direction of the Pacific Ocean.

The messengers and town councillors picked up the luggage. So I grabbed the post-bag, and Leslie carried the radio. It had been so good to see the pilot after several weeks out of touch with the base, and now, with the radio, we would have a daily link again. The post-bag was very welcome too, with its news from England, as the Tataltepec address was only just coming into use. The president said that some letters had come with the last delivery, and he had kept them in safety for us at the Town Hall, so Leslie could collect them officially that evening.

The procession moved off towards our house, and we could hear much speculation among the crowd, in both Spanish and Chatino, as to what all the things were that comprised so much cargo. The men carried everything inside, and Leslie offered them a tip, but they said, no, they were on duty at the Town Hall, and the president had sent them. Later, Leslie delivered an official invitation at the

Town Hall to all who had helped carry, to come and drink coffee with us the next evening.

Meanwhile, we got the stove unpacked and fixed up. There was only one other metal stove in Tataltepec, and that was run on paraffin, and belonged to a shop-keeper. The president's family all came to view this marvel, and were very impressed by the little oven (made from soldered biscuit tins) that sat on top. The radio came next, and the president's older sons were only too glad to help with fixing up the aerial. At the same time I unpacked the medicines, and tried to sort out the other boxes. The oven crate made a very good wash-bowl stand, and the stove crate was soon converted into shelves. Leslie had bought a number of seven-foot-long boards and some bricks locally, so we made two sets of shelves with them — one for books, papers and office things, and the other for clothes, etc. From our previous experience of adobe houses, I knew how useful pretty curtains are, so I had collected a stock. Now we curtained off the darkest end of the house in two sections for washroom and bedroom. Then we made shelves underneath the stove table and the medicine table, and hung curtain skirts round them. The kitchen area had a stack of packing-case shelves with another curtain, and the house began to look quite gay and lived-in. The little oven proved its worth the day after our arrival, as I made a mountain of rock buns and banana bread ready for the evening.

A group of younger town messengers, plus a couple of councillors, arrived to drink coffee. All were Chatinos. We had observed that all the general stores served whisky and other drink. We had also noticed that when men ordered drinks, they usually ordered music as well. Several stores had a stack of popular records, a record player, a small generator to run it, and a loud-speaker which was fixed up on a pole or a tree outside, so that everyone in town could share in the drinker's choice. We thought it might be a good idea to show that music does not have to be associated with hard drinking, so Leslie put a music tape on the tape-recorder. The wonders of the tape-recorder entertained people for a little while, and then there was the Tilley lamp. The Town Hall had a pressure lamp, but it ran only on white petrol, which is twice as expensive as the paraffin fuel for the Tilley. Leslie passed round *Geographic* magazines, and we were kept busy trying to answer their questions as they looked at the pictures. We learnt a lot of new words too, and that provided more entertainment as we tried to write down some of those new words. The coffee and cake seemed to meet with approval, and then I heard the oldest man say quietly to a young man next to him:

'Where's the whisky bottle, then?'

'Oh, these people don't have any,' was the reply.

I looked more closely at the young man then. How did he know so surely? That was how we met Leo, and we later discovered what a gifted young man he was.

When they had finished, they politely returned their cups, each one formally thanking me. Then they left, and we hoped that they knew a little more about us. We did not realise until much later how brave that group had been to come and eat and drink at our house in the face of all the gossip and dire rumours that were flying round the town at that time.

With our boxes unpacked and our house set up, we decided that we needed to look for consistent language help. So I went back to visit the family in the very first house where we had been introduced on the day of our arrival. They seemed glad to see me, and were eager for me to write down what they said. The daughter-in-law was doing some embroidery and wanted to know about the Yaitepec women's embroidery, so I said that I would come again the next day and bring a paper about it. They were fascinated when they saw the embroidery booklets, and bought one so that they could use the patterns. I gradually realised that the other young woman who was usually present was, in fact, a cousin, and lived in another little house just across the trail with her father, grandmother and small daughter. This was Inés, and one day I went to her own home, and gradually worked round to the question of whether she would like to come and work for me for two hours each afternoon, to help me learn the language. She lived near the school, so I suggested that she should come when the children went into afternoon school (three p.m.), and then she would always know the time. She jumped at the chance, as she had no husband and her father was a terrible drunkard. She and her ancient grandmother worked very hard to get enough to eat each day, and their tiny house was badly in need of repair, so any additional income was very welcome.

Leslie went to see Juvencio on the same mission, and he agreed to come every morning for two or three hours, before breakfast, so that he would not lose any working time in his cornfield. He usually arrived between five and six a.m., but one brilliant moonlight night, he woke up, and was sure that it was dawn, so he hurried over to our house to work. Gradually we became aware of this quiet but insistent voice greeting us from the porch:

'Are you asleep? Are you *still* asleep?'

Groaning, Leslie went to let him in, and put on the kettle for a cup of coffee — it was three a.m.! I went back to sleep, but they worked four-and-a-half hours that morning, and Leslie was ravenous by breakfast time.

The rest of the day we attended to people who came for medicine, chatted with other visitors, went out to visit people to buy something (usually food) or because they were ill, and worked at our language data in between times. We had to sort out the sounds and analyse the structure to find out how the words and expressions fitted together. This helped us to catch on to one or two basic patterns in which the Tataltepec language differed from the mountain Chatino. Then we were able to formulate some rough 'rules' which enabled us to quickly translate from our mountain Chatino memory store into the Tataltepec language. We tried this out on Juvencio and Inés, and they were delighted by our quick progress. Sometimes we drew a blank, though. I wanted to ask Inés about a hen, one day. Now, the mountain Chatino word is *kwitu*, so I made what we thought were the predictable changes, and asked her about a kityu. She looked very puzzled, and reminded me that 'paper' is *kityi* . . . So I found a picture of a hen:

'What is the name of this?' I asked her.

'*Su'u*,' she replied. 'Is that the thing you wanted? Why did you say that funny word kityu then?'

'I am learning very slowly, and I keep making mistakes,' I said. The complete answer was just too technical to explain.

One morning, I found a woman on our porch just sitting quietly, but obviously in pain. At my question, she brought her hand out from under her shawl, and showed me the thumb swollen and red. It looked ready to burst at the slightest provocation, and the skin was all shiny where the corrugations were pushed out and stretched. She told me that the whole arm ached right up to her shoulder.

'Yes, there is a root in my armpit,' she said. 'I got a thorn in my thumb a few days ago, and I took it out with a needle. It was such a relief for one day, then it got red like this and began to hurt again, so I came to see if you have any medicine, because I can't make my tortillas with it like this.'

I told her that she would need an injection to kill the root, and that there was pus inside from the infection.

'Oh no! I got the thorn out, and the hole healed up. There's no pus in it. It's just red swelling, and that's dangerous. But go ahead and inject me to kill the root, and please do something about the swelling.'

I gave her Veganin for the pain and a series of penicillin injections, while I treated the thumb locally. She was amazed when it burst the next day and great quantities of puss came out. That was our first encounter with Chona, and from that day on she was very convinced of the efficacy of modern medicine for herself and her family. She agreed to make a daily supply of tortillas for us and that she, or one of the children, would deliver them at dinner time each day. As she got more used to us, she began to ask questions about our families and our home country.

'Is your mother still alive?' she enquired. I produced our family snapshots, and she and other visitors never tired of examining them. In fact, we were both getting lots of practice in one standard conversation, and consequently becoming very fluent in the answers, both in Chatino and Spanish. It went like this:

'The shop-keeper says you are Americans from the north.'

'No, the pilot is an American, and lots of our friends are Americans, but we are English, and we come from the other side of the sea.'

'You don't come from the north then, where Don Chico went to work once?'

'No, we come from England.'

'How did you come, and how long does it take?'

'From here, we first have to go to the north, to America, by road. It takes nearly a week on the bus to go from here right through the home-land of the Americans to the edge of the sea at New York. Then we go in a big boat for another week, and when we get to the other side, we just go a few hours on the bus to get to our home-towns.'

'Do you both come from the same place, and do your parents still live there?'

'Yes, our parents are still alive and living in their own homes, but in different places, because we don't both come from the same home-town. In fact, we come from little villages, and my father is a farmer.'

'Oh, what animals does he have, and how big is his cornfield?'

'He has a few cattle and some chicken, but he doesn't grow maize corn like you do here. Not much maize grows in our country because it's too cold, and the sun doesn't shine enough. They grow wheat for flour instead.'

'How do you make tortillas then, if there's no maize?'

'English people have never seen tortillas. They eat salt bread made from flour.'

Wonderingly: 'How *do* they survive? Does that give men enough strength to work, then?'

'Yes, the men work — they like the salt bread.'

We usually showed people some pictures of England at this point, to help them to take in both the similarities to, and the differences from, their own locality. We could not understand why people went away so puzzled, and why the same people kept asking the same questions. Then, one day Leslie asked an old man about the sea. The only sea he knew of was the Pacific Ocean, which he had seen once.

'There are four seas,' he said. 'The first one, by the shore, is salt water, and when you get through that, you come to the Mud Sea. Then you go on to the Sea of Blood, and beyond that is the Sea of Pitch, which no one can get through. They say you come from the other side of the sea. Can a big "wood-house" (boat) really go through that pitch? Is there really more water on the other side, and how do people live on water?'

No wonder people thought we were a bit strange, with so many conflicting 'facts' to sort out and reconcile in their minds.

Another day, a little girl of about nine or ten years old brought a watermelon to sell. We sat on the porch, agreed on a price, and just chatted. Suddenly she said:

'It isn't true, is it?'

'What isn't true?' I asked in surprise.

'That you eat dead children?'

'No, of course not. Whoever said that? We are just ordinary human beings, and whoever heard of people who eat dead children?'

'That's what I thought, so I said I was going to come and ask you. You remember that child's funeral yesterday? Well, somebody said that you went out to the graveyard last night and dug up the coffin to eat the corpse, so the parents have gone out there to check now, and to see if they can find your footprints near the grave.'

I felt a little sick as I realised that some people really believed this kind of thing, and I marvelled at this little girl's temerity at coming to ask me straight out. I assured her that we had slept soundly all night, and that if we really wanted people to die, we would not bother to give them medicine to stay alive. Then I tried to tell her why we had come, and why we cared about the people of Tataltepec.

One morning, a lovely young girl appeared. She was not well, and had tried various local cures without success, but she had never had an injection. She had heard that we gave injections, so perhaps our medicine would help her. As I pieced together the symptoms, it became more and more evident that she probably had tuberculosis, and we only had one of the necessary medicines with us in those early days. This girl, Macrina, came faithfully for injections twice or three times a week all that summer, and seemed to be a bit better. We determined to find out more about tuberculosis and its treatment, and to come back better prepared next time.

The president's three little boys continued to haunt our house. They were fascinated by the *Geographic* magazines. The older two were also intrigued by the gas stove. I had taught the nine-year-old to light it, which he did with alacrity and great satisfaction every time I needed it. They also loved to help me mix things. Great was their joy when I made American pancakes one evening, and let one of them put the batter in the pan, spoonful by spoonful, while the other one turned them, and lifted them out when they were cooked. They tried one and seemed to like it, so I sent them home with a little bowlful for the family, which they carried off triumphantly. Their mother returned the bowl in the morning, and told me with a laugh that they were absolutely bursting with pride of achievement. In fact they had made their sister quite jealous. Would it be too much to ask me to teach her to make cakes, as they all enjoyed the things I had given them from time to time? So we made banana bread together, and chocolate rock buns, using local chocolate made from home-grown cacao. Her cowboy brother mashed the bananas for us, and chopped up the little cakes of chocolate to my amazement.

These two were very conscious of their limited education, so they got the president to ask us if we would help them to study in the evenings for an hour. We assured him that we would gladly help his children to study anatomy, hygiene, food values and so on, as this would help the general health of their family, and be of help to the whole town. We taught them about parasites too, and how to use the medicines available at the general stores, and finally to give injections. With this limited knowledge, they were able to help quite a lot of people. As they wanted to study, we tried to introduce them to the Bible too, and urged on them the importance of the New Testament as a textbook for our lives.

One afternoon I was quietly working with Inés, when I became aware of the scuffling of feet, and lots of giggling and whispering coming from the porch.

'Is dinner cooked?'

'Yes, dinner is very cooked,' I replied. Then I went out on to the porch to face a bevy of bright teenage girls. One boldly asked to look at magazines, so I handed them out, and called Inés out to join us, as this was the first time that any group of older girls had come to visit us. They immediately quizzed her on what work she did for me, and how much I paid her, at the same time asking me lots of questions about the pictures. My attention was caught especially by one very quick and vivacious girl who was obviously a leader among them. When the others giggled at my mistakes as I tried to answer their questions, she frowned and told them off, her bright eyes flashing.

'Don't just giggle; correct her, so that she can learn the language quickly. The Spanish-speakers don't bother to learn our language, so we should help people who do try.' After this speech I was even more attracted to her — that was my first meeting with Florida.

Now the time was coming to leave for a few weeks, and as we packed I took stock. (This packing up always takes time as those same old anti-rat, anti-damp precautions must be observed for anything left in the house.) I thought how easy our coming to Tataltepec had been, how everything had been all ready, and how friendly people had been. The more educated Spanish-speakers had wanted to absorb us into their stratum of the local society, but God had helped us to quickly get into the local Chatino language, to make friends among the more acceptable well-to-do Chatino people, and among the poor, despised and rejected families, as well as remaining good friends with our Spanish-speaking neighbours and the headmaster of the school. It was a further confirmation that we were working according to His plan. However, there was still one all-Chatino and very conservative corner of the town that we didn't seem to have had any contact with. We had no means of knowing if any of the people living there had visited us or not, but we had certainly not visited any homes there.

Everything was ready, and we would dismantle the radio after a final weather report to the pilot in the morning. We awoke to the familiar:

'Are you asleep?'

Surely Juvencio had not forgotten that we were leaving? But it did not really sound like his voice, and it was only three a.m. Leslie went to the door.

'I'm so sorry to disturb you, but could your wife possibly come? My wife says the pains are very bad, and she is very afraid because we only have one living child. She said to remind you that she had been coming for the vitamin injections, and has taken all the pills you gave her, and the Old Lady promised that she would come day or night.'

I was fully awake now.

'Is that Anatolia?' I asked, as I crawled out from under the mosquito net.

'That's right, Vidal's mother,' he said.

Leslie had the agitated man sit down, and in a few minutes we were both dressed, and had collected a sterile syringe and what we had in the way of maternity equipment. We both went back with him, and found ourselves in 'Here Down Below'. This was that especially conservative corner of town that we had wondered about. We approached a small house with a bee-hive shaped adobe bread oven outside, under its own little roof. Anatolia was walking up and down inside, and even as we entered she knelt down on a dirty sack in the corner as another labour pain gripped her. Five-year-old Vidal was asleep on the bed, and Anatolia's mother sat beside him. Anatolia herself was wearing her usual clothes, and had her black shawl tied round her head. I timed the pains, took her pulse and temperature, and asked what preparations had been made for the new baby. Granny seemed to be satisfied of my capability by these attentions, and said she would take the sleeping child to her house so that he would not be frightened if he woke — I think she meant, by us — but she would come back if we needed her. The fire was built up, and as we settled down to wait, I silently prayed, rather desperately, wishing I had even one quarter the confidence that Granny seemed to have in me. Then we prayed with Anatolia and her husband for God's help to strengthen her, and for His mercy on them, that they would have another healthy child. They seemed very grateful for this prayer, but were amazed that it was directed straight to God Himself, and in Chatino words. Then the crisis came, and at least there was a clean cloth on top of the dirty sack on that earth floor, as that new baby boy made his debut into a loving family circle but a very hostile environment. To my relief, he began to cry lustily which brought Granny back at a run, and together we got mother and baby attended to and tucked up in bed to rest. I told them that I would get the president's daughter to come and give Anatolia some more vitamin B injections, and I gave her some more pills. Then we thanked God together for His gift to them, and that was another eye-opener for them.

Leslie and I went home rejoicing. We looked up at the feathery palms outlined against the orange glow of the dawn sky, and we were walking on air. This could only be the Lord God Omnipotent's doing, that after just three months here, we had been given this highest vote of confidence —

we had been invited to help at the most intimately guarded family secret, the birth of a new baby. We knew that no one outside the family could see that infant for many weeks to come, as he would stay in the security of his own home. Unrelated visitors to the house would not be invited in. Even relatives if thought to be untrustworthy while allowed in would see only a bundle of cloth, and a handkerchief covering the child's face.

Yes, we would be back in a few weeks, and we eagerly looked forward to having the alphabet all worked out, and to the start of Bible translation in Tataltepec Chatino.

8

The First Book

Leslie continued working with Juvencio in the early mornings, and I worked with Inés in the afternoons. We recorded Chatino stories on the tape-recorder from anyone who would tell one into the machine, and groups of men and boys were constant visitors in the evenings to hear these story tapes played back. To get them all written down took a long time. Sorting out the actual meaning of each word was a slow process, but it taught us both a lot more about the language and about the thought patterns of the people. After a little experience, Leslie worked through them all with Juvencio first, particularly those told by the men, as some were so obscene that he would not let me hear them. They were promptly eliminated from the repertoire played for our visitors.

Since people loved to hear the 'radio that speaks Chatino', Leslie and Juvencio worked out a simple presentation of the Gospel message, including Genesis, chapter 1, and Juvencio agreed to tell it 'into the machine'. People listened carefully when this new tape was played, and we hoped that it would counteract some of the traditional legends about the beginning of the world, and about Jesus Christ, the poor but magical person who performed all kinds of capricious acts, often at the instigation of the devil.

This was all good preparation for translation. We had

been advised to tackle a 'Life of Christ' first, made up of passages from the four Gospels, selected and recommended by the Bible Society. We divided the passages between us for initial translation, and then we worked over what the other one had done, each with our own Chatino helpers. Next, Leslie typed up this rather rough version, and took it with him to visit one or two elderly friends. He read it to them, and got their reactions — their comments and questions helped to improve the draft a bit.

One of his elderly advisors was Arnulfo, who was a respected man of substance, as he owned pigs, cattle, a few mules, coffee, sugar cane, coconut trees and some good irrigated land. The family also had a bread oven, and they sold sweet rolls that they made in it. It was not just his riches that had gained him respect; he had been a member of the town council several times, and he had completed all the offices of religious host to the annual fiestas, so he had earned the title of town 'elder'. This old man listened carefully to the Gospel stories, and made many helpful suggestions and improvements. He told Leslie excitedly that, as a child, the schoolteacher had told them such stories of Jesus Christ, but he could not remember them any more, and he had never heard them again till now. He tried hard to understand their significance, but he was very frail and old. Then he became ill, and he asked to record an ancient Chatino song on tape. This was the first time we had been able to trace any indigenous Chatino music, but we were chilled as we worked out the words. It was a lament to the effect that everyone grows old, and all must die, but no one knows the way beyond death, so all are lost and helpless.

Leslie redoubled his efforts to help this attractive old man see the personal application to himself of the Gospel stories in which he showed so much interest, but he died moaning that it was very dark, and he did not know the way.

This put a new spur to the flanks of our translation efforts, and we thought it was time we got some expert help. It was arranged that we should meet a senior translation consultant at the centre in Mitla, and she would check over with us what we had done. We would need a Chatino-speaker with us, of course, but who would trust us enough to go?

Our gifted young friend Leo had often come with other friends in the evening to look at magazines and ask questions, to listen to the 'radio that speaks Chatino', or to see how we were getting on with writing down the language. Worms were such a medical problem, that we had made a poster and stuck it up on the wall. It gave a life-history of the roundworm in both Chatino and Spanish, with illustrations. The first time Leo saw it, he walked over to it, and with only occasional prompting read all the Chatino written there. This was most encouraging to us because it helped to confirm the choice of letters for the Chatino alphabet, and also showed us that here was someone who wanted to learn. He had little opportunity to fulfil his ambition, as he worked hard in the fields with his father all day. Leo was old Arnulfo's great-nephew.

One evening he brought his cousin Cresenciano with him. We wondered why just the two of them had come that evening, and after the usual chat and questions, Leo asked:

'Do you have any medicine for lumps?'

'What do you mean, "lumps"?'

'Well, like this. Take your shirt off, Cresenciano.'

We looked at the young man's back, and there on the shoulder-blade was a lump like half an egg. It was very hard, and all one piece, but we had to tell them that the only medicine for that was surgery.

'People do live after the surgeon cuts them, don't they?' said Cresenciano then. 'I really do want to get rid of this lump. It doesn't hurt or anything, but it's an embarrassing blemish.'

We assured him that people did live afterwards. In fact, 'the surgeon had cut' me twice, and here I was, alive to tell the tale. Leslie told him that it would have to be done in the state capital, Oaxaca City, and asked him if he was willing to stay in the hospital there by himself. He said that he was, if he could go to Mitla with us. Was this the man to be our translation helper? We had never worked with him before. Leslie told him that we would think over the whole matter, and then he would go and talk to his parents. Cresenciano explained where they lived, and it turned out that he was also a cousin of Juvencio's and lived next door to him, although the two families were often not on speaking terms. We thought that if he had only half the intelligence of his cousin Leo, he would be an excellent language and translation helper. We also knew that he needed attention for that lump soon, and we wanted to help.

Leslie went round to discuss the matter with his parents, and to explain the situation plainly to them about doctors, surgeons, hospitals and fees. We would pay his way in the plane, if he would work with us in the preparation of this book. We would pay him wages for the days he worked with us, and he could live with us, so that would not be an expense. We would take him to the doctor initially, but the hospital bill would be their responsibility. They were anxious about their son, and agreed to this plan.

It was now a year since we had first arrived in Tataltepec — as, at one point, we had been away for several months helping in a training programme for new members — and Inés was no longer able to work with me, so I was looking out for another steady helper. Early one morning, while Leslie and Juvencio were still at work, I found a small man sitting on our porch smoking a home-made cigar — tobacco is another locally grown item. He asked if I would visit his daughter who was too ill to move.

'We have given her all the medicine that we know of, but she just gets worse,' he said. I told him that Leslie was busy, and I could not come just at that moment, but if someone would show me the way later in the morning, I would come.

'My other daughter will come to fetch you,' he said. 'I must go out to work now, but don't worry about the money, I shall pay you.'

Later on the daughter came, and I found myself following

her over to 'Here Down Below' again. Suddenly she turned on the trail and said,

'Macrina died.'

I could not believe my ears. We had wondered why that beautiful girl with T.B. had not reappeared for the new medicine we had brought back with us, but that was many months ago now.

'Did you say Macrina?' I asked.

'Yes, dead—Macrina is my sister. She died while you were away so long. She was better after she had the injections last summer, so she didn't bother to come for the new medicine in the autumn. Then she got much worse after you left again, and coughed up blood every morning. Lots of witch-doctors and curers came, but they didn't help at all, and she kept saying that she should have listened to you, and that she was afraid to die.'

Soon we arrived at a typical Tataltepec house, with pole walls. It was right at the edge of town, and there on a mat on the floor sat the vivacious girl with the flashing eyes that I had been so attracted to before — this was Florida. I recognised her only because of those eyes, the ready smile and the quick wit, for her body was wasted away to just skin and bone, except for a bulbous, great, swollen knee.

'Why, it's you!' I exclaimed. I had not known her name, or where she lived, till now, and it was obvious why she had not been again to our house.

'Yes, I'm me. Do you have any medicine?'

I saw the running sores on her neck, heard the wracking cough, and felt the burning fever and galloping pulse. I tried not to weep as I asked *why* they had not told me sooner — we had been back several weeks. They agreed to one month's course of medicine, so I made daily visits to the house from then on.

That first weekend was a terrible crisis, with all the symptoms intensified, and Florida prostrate. I went twice on both the Saturday and the Sunday, and I was terribly afraid that they would give up and call in the witch-doctor again.

Almost in tears, again I prayed with them in the faltering Chatino of those early days, and on Monday she was a little better. We weighed her then — four stones seven pounds at seventeen years old! I knew that a miracle was needed for her recovery. At the end of the month the crisis was over, the glands in the neck were healing, the cough was less, and she was making progress. That was the end of it, they thought, she will get better now, and anyway, there is no more money for medicine. I had often taken a pencil and paper with me, and had found her to be a ready and intelligent helper with my language difficulties. Now I proposed that I come every afternoon for an hour to 'work with paper', and in exchange I would provide her with further medicine. I began to work on translating some more of those passages from the Gospels with her too, and sometimes the whole family were there listening and chipping in with suggestions. We also started literacy lessons for a short time each day, and she proved a very apt pupil. She had started school late, and then with her mother's illness and death, she had been constantly needed at home, so her schooldays added up to just a few non-consecutive weeks. She was thrilled to find that she could actually learn. Her father too was impressed to see that the Chatino language could be written down and actually be read from the paper by his own un-lettered daughter.

Florida had been only nine, and Macrina twelve years old, when their mother died, leaving six children. Their father decided to keep the family together, so he helped these two older daughters to cook. The eldest child was a boy of fourteen, and he went to the fields to work with his father. Four years later, Macrina married, and her husband had been a real help to his father-in-law until he was ill. Then Macrina herself had become ill, and we knew the rest. Her stricken, young husband had returned to his own parents' home soon after the funeral. The eldest boy had married a few months before his sister's death, and lived just across the yard, so he still worked with his father. I recognised his giggling young wife as another of that crowd of girls that had visited us with Florida.

As I got to know this fun-loving, cheerful family, I saw that the younger brother also had suppurating glands in his neck, was very under-sized for his age, and had a slight cough. I pointed all this out to his father, who asked him if he wanted any medicine. A very subdued boy went and sat dejectedly in the corner of the house, alone, refusing to answer. He was desperately afraid of medicine, especially injections, and his father would not force him. So, four years later, he too was dead.

In the meantime, the day was fast approaching for us to go to Mitla with Cresenciano to check the translation we had done. I pleaded with the family for Florida to go too, so that she could see the doctor, and continue with the medicine, but to no avail. They were afraid of the plane flight, and they were afraid she would die away from home. I was afraid she would die in our absence, like her sister, but finally, I left an adequate stock of oral medicine with her, and we went to the base at Mitla.

The Scripture stories were entirely new to Cresenciano, and at times he was completely mystified. With the guidance of the consultant each day we both learnt a lot about translation technique. With constant question and answer, the meaning became clearer to Cresenciano, and he was able to help us improve on the Chatino version yet again. It took ten days to get through those first translated passages, with a lot of private tutoring from that very helpful and patient consultant, and Cresenciano ended up with quite a different idea of desk work — that one actually gets tired 'just sitting and looking at paper all day', he discovered!

The doctor had said that the lump was just a surface bone tumour so far as he could tell, but gave us an introduction to his friend who was a bone specialist and consultant surgeon at the Civil Hospital in Oaxaca City. Sure enough, the great man did the operation himself, and it was very successful. On careful examination, they found the tumour to be benign, as had been suspected. Leslie had been told to collect the patient on the tenth day, but Cresenciano made such good progress that they were ready to discharge him on the ninth day. He asked the social worker who interviewed him for information about the buses to Mitla, assured them that he could manage, and would return for his check-up in five days' time. We were amazed when he jauntily walked in, and said:

'You won't have to come for me tomorrow, Leslie, because they let me come early. I did all that they said, and got better very quickly, because they gave us such tiny tortillas to eat, that I almost starved! Do you have any real tortillas? I'm hungry!'

While he recuperated, he helped me with some preliminary work on literacy materials. Like his cousin Leo, he very quickly adapted to reading and writing his own language, and began to get quite interested in the idea of a Chatino book. Leslie was now typing up the improved draft of the translation, and we wished that Cresenciano would show some spark of interest in the content of that manuscript, but he was much more taken up with the idea of a story book, or a book for learning Spanish.

On our return to Tataltepec, we worked through the manuscript once more with Juvencio and Florida, and then pushed on to translate the rest of the Life of Christ selection. Our hearts were full of praise to see Florida, who had faithfully taken the medicine in our absence. Her knee was back to its normal size, and she was able to walk without a limp; she had gained about half-a-stone in weight and was eating well; the open ulcers on her neck had healed, and the hard lumps in her glands were decreasing; while her temperature was normal most of the time now, and she only coughed in the evening and first thing in the morning, but never with blood.

At last we were ready to see the translation consultant again — this time with the completed manuscript. It was arranged that we should go to our headquarters in Mexico

City on this occasion, and we wondered who would be willing to go that far with us. We were quite surprised to find that Juvencio was very willing to go. He had been unwell for some time, and this was quite a worry to him, with a growing family of little daughters to feed. He just did not have the strength to 'last out' all day working in his cornfield, and he had frequent, vague, abdominal symptoms, as well as headaches. He wanted to know if we would take him to the doctor, like his cousin Cresenciano.

So it was that Juvencio came with us, and, after tests, got treated for various intestinal parasites, including hookworm. The regular, good food helped too, although it was a big adjustment for him to eat with us and everyone else in the central dining room. He was terribly out of his element in that big city atmosphere, as well as being miserably cold because of the altitude. We soon found him some warm clothes, but he clung to us as the only links with his home. His limited Spanish increased his natural inferiority complex, and he made no effort to mix with the other translation helpers there at that time, although one or two tried to be friendly. He did not want to sleep with them, so we divided up our room with the wardrobe, and put him behind it in a bed in the corner. We began to realise that it was a great mistake to take anyone as introspective as Juvencio away from home without a Chatino companion, but we could hardly remedy that now.

There was the bath problem. Our room had a shower and toilet leading off it and, unlike some of the other translation helpers, Juvencio had no problem learning to cope with a flushing toilet. The shower was a different matter. The Tataltepec Chatino people are in the habit of having a bath almost every day. Most of them go to the river with a gourd, and throw water over themselves, then soap all over, and throw more gourds of water over themselves to rinse off, so we thought that he would appreciate the similarity of the water showering down, and would like the improvement that it came automatically. We were wrong. We found that when laundry day was approaching, and Leslie would again have to remind him to have a bath, so that I could wash his dirty clothes.

One morning I had reserved an hour to use the washing machine, and Juvencio said it was too cold first thing, he would have a bath after breakfast. Afterwards I waited a bit irritably, and I could hear the water being turned on and off, on and off. Why ever did he use the shower like that?

'I just wonder if he is only using cold water, and that's why he doesn't want to have a bath!' exclaimed Leslie. 'No wonder he's cold if that's it, but I showed him how to mix the hot and cold water.'

The mournful-eyed little man came out, and handed me his neatly rolled bundle of clothes without a word, and I dashed off before my reservation on the machine ran out.

'I'm going outside in the sun. It's freezing in here,' said Juvencio to Leslie as he made for the door. Leslie went out with him, agreeing that Mexico City was indeed cold like all places so high up in the mountains.

'That's why they have hot water for baths,' said Leslie. 'I could never last out without warm water here or in my own country.'

'Really?' said Juvencio, amazed. 'Do you use hot water for your bath, then?'

'Always,' said Leslie. 'So does everyone else around here, so that they don't catch cold. Don't you use hot water then —I thought I showed you how to do it, but perhaps I didn't?'

'Oh yes, you showed me how to turn both taps on and to mix the water, but I thought that was just for people who were ill. People say that if you use hot water for a bath, your skin will soon dry up, and you will get a fever and be very ill. People who are well always use only cold water.'

Leslie explained that this was fine for a hot tropical place down in a coconut grove, but it was quite different in a cold place high in the mountains, and you had to follow the local customs. In this case that meant hot baths. Juvencio's next bath was hot, and he waited in fear and trepidation for the next few days for illness to strike. When it did not, after his second hot bath, he was emancipated, and decided to have a hot shower every morning, so that he would be warm to face the day. Now, we sometimes had to bang on the bathroom door to get him to come out so that we could get to breakfast on time!

The checking was finished, and Juvencio's health was much better, so he began worrying about his family and his fields. Leslie decided to take him home, and then to come back and re-type the manuscript one last time ready for the publications department. There were a few other things that we needed to catch up on, and it would be good to have a little holiday too. We selected the pictures; we chose the paper and the type-style, and decided on the cover; we discussed the page arrangement — this was to be a diglot publication with both the Chatino and Spanish versions on the same page; finally we handed over the manuscript. Of course, the publications department had lots of other books of various sorts and sizes, and in many different languages, waiting to be printed. So it took some months for the *Life of Christ* to eventually come off the press. What a thrill it was to receive that first book in the Tataltepec Chatino language. We marvelled at its potential, and looked forward to what the Holy Spirit would do through it.

9

Day by Day

WE RETURNED TO Tataltepec from Mexico City, to await the arrival of the book. I was concentrating on a book for teaching people to read, and other literacy aids, while Leslie was doing some more linguistic investigation.

One day Leslie was called to see a man who lived in a most disreputable little shack, more tumbledown than any house we had seen. His wife and two little children were with him. He had been ill for many months and was suffering from the usual malnutrition as a result of the extreme dieting that had been imposed upon him by his curers. The whole family had very little to eat so that the children too were in a sad state of malnutrition and internal parasites. This was Taurino, who became our very good friend and counsellor.

Unlike most of our friends, he did not seem to be related to anyone else. He did not seem to have many close friends either, because he was a non-conformist in many things, a thinker and an innovator. This is unforgivable in a closed society, where every custom must be faithfully perpetuated and never questioned, and change from within is not to be tolerated.

He and his children soon began to respond to treatment, and he was fascinated by that one Chatino book which had now arrived. He had never had the chance to go to school, so he had Leslie read the stories to him, and he associated them with the pictures and asked endless questions. Soon he was able to go out and do light work again, which gave the family new hope.

We had long wanted to move because our house was so noisy when the loud-speakers were blaring, and was very damp in the rainy season. Now, what we considered to be a much more convenient house became available, right next door to Taurino. So we moved into it. There was a little bit of land with this house, so at last we were able to dig a deep toilet hole, and to start a little vegetable garden. Taurino proved to himself and everyone else that he really was better by digging that hole for us through solid sandstone. He also earned some money and paid off his medical bill in the process. Then he dug a wide, shallow hole for the garden, and filled it with wheelbarrow loads of fertile soil from a little gully thirty yards away. He took a great interest in the radishes, carrots and cabbages that we planted and experimented with some of the seed for himself. The family learnt to like radishes and cabbages especially, and he was willing to look after our little garden in our absence. Soon he was able to get together the necessary materials, and to rebuild his house, which gave them all a new sense of well-being.

Later, when he was ill again, he took the opportunity to teach himself to read, on the days when he was not in much pain. He learnt to read in Spanish from his daughter's school books, and in Chatino from our reading primer, which was now in print. The next thing we knew, he was reading the *Life of Christ* for himself, and asking new questions. He also discovered the horticultural lessons in the schoolbooks, and, after asking Leslie a few questions about them to make sure that he had understood the Spanish, he was convinced of their validity. He was the only Chatino that we have met who had ever realised the relevance of such information to his own life and farming methods, and as soon as he was better, he started in a small way to put some of this advice into practice. This attitude also meant that he asked more searching questions about the Scriptures than anyone else, and when he was convinced, he put it into practice.

One day when Chona brought our tortillas, she said:

'I don't think I will be able to make the tortillas tomorrow morning. Do you still want them if my daughter makes them? She is quite good at it now.'

'Yes, please. Are you going away or something?'

'No, but the pain is getting worse — you will come when it is time, won't you?'

Light dawned. She was expecting a baby, and we had been building up her strength a bit with vitamins and iron. Now the labour pains had started.

'Let me give you one more injection for strength now, and then you let me know when the big pains start coming close together.'

'Yes, the injections do help. But you will come, won't you, even if it's the middle of the night?'

'Yes, I'll come. Now, you should buy a brand new razor blade to cut the cord, and make the strings ready — I need two. Then we need several clean cloths for the baby. It doesn't matter how old they are, but brand new people need clean things.'

So it happened that we were awakened in the night.

'Are you asleep? Are you asleep?'

'Yes, we're asleep!'

'Please forgive me for waking you up, but could the Old Woman come now because my children's mother is having very severe pains.'

I recognised Delfino's quiet voice and leapt out of bed. To do this speedily in an emergency is quite an art, when you have to untuck the mosquito net and find the torch first, especially if your husband is doing the same thing on the other side! I asked Delfino who was with Chona.

'She didn't want me to tell anyone else as you were coming, so I left her alone. The children are sleeping with my mother tonight.'

It doesn't take many minutes to dress in the tropics, and,

Leslie was checking through the medical bag at the same time. Then Delfino was leading the way with a stick to ward off people's watch-dogs, which sometimes become quite savage at night when they are roused from sleep.

We arrived at their tiny home to find Chona kneeling on a small mat in the corner, and her husband had not exaggerated about the severe pains. I quickly checked: 'You have clean cloths for receiving the baby?'

'Yes.'

'And a new razor blade from the store for cutting the cord?'

'Yes.'

'What shall we tie off the cord with?'

'I don't know — we forgot about that.'

'Do you have some cotton thread?'

'Yes, my mother just spun some the other day,' responded Delfino.

'Well, make two strings about so long (a foot) and ten strands of cotton to each.'

He quickly but carefully rolled the threads together, and the strings were ready. He then blew up the fire in the kitchen, and put some water on to heat, for me to scrub my hands.

I had just done so when Chona called to her husband in a frightened voice: 'The pain is much worse now. I think the baby is coming, so please hold me.'

He sat behind her and supported her round the waist. There was a splash and a plop, and I searched under her skirt quickly to grab the feet of this brand new bit of humanity. He gave a hearty yell, and a relieved and proud smile came over the faces of his parents as I told them it was a healthy big boy — a pocket edition of Delfino in fact.

'Now what will his name be?' I asked, after mother and baby were comfortably tucked up for the rest of the night.

'Who knows?' said his father.

'I wonder?' said his mother, and, then to me, 'Do you have a calendar?'

Now, we don't hold any brief in defence of the Mexican almanac of (Catholic) saints, the mainstay of countless rural superstitions, but it is the local custom to name a child from this almanac, and we thought that, having a copy of our own was a harmless way of empathising with the people (and of making sure that the town secretary did not put one over on them if he was drunk when they registered a new birth!) I said that I would bring it the next day when I came to see them.

Next morning we looked up the baby's birth date in the calendar of saints and found Rodrigo. That evening Delfino went to the Town Hall to report the baby's birth to the secretary, who in turn looked at the calendar and informed Delfino that his new son's name was indeed Rodrigo. So Rodrigo was officially registered as a new junior citizen of Tataltepec.

Grannie Victoria was one of the most elderly citizens of Tataltepec, and remembered much of a past generation. She had been a widow for many years, and lived alone in her own adobe house, although her son Delfino, and his brother, with their respective families, lived in houses not a stone's throw away, so she had plenty of company. She was full of good humour, often laughing and joking, and her daughters-in-law showed her great respect and seemed to be very fond of her. She wore the old-fashioned ankle-length, wrap-around skirt secured by a girdle, and good-naturedly accepted the teasing of the younger members of the family who dress in more modern style.

Soon after the arrival of the Chatino records made by a Gospel Recordings team who visited Tataltepec, Chona came to ask us if we could take the machine over to their house to play them, as Granny Victoria had heard about these Chatino records, and could hardly believe that there were such things. That afternoon I carefully arranged my shawl (such as all country women wear in Mexico) so that it covered my burden, and went to visit Granny Victoria (These shawls seem to be worn as much to hide one's errand from inquisitive neighbours as for any other kind of protection, although they are very convenient for carrying young children). Almost by radar it seemed that the whole family was alerted, so that sons, daughters-in-law, daughter and grandchildren all gathered at Granny's house to hear the records. The adults sat on Granny's bed and long narrow benches along the walls, and the children sat on straw mats on the floor. I was told to use the family altar table for the machine, and all listened very attentively. I paused at the end of each side of a record, and they discussed it among themselves — Granny Victoria pronounced them 'good words', so we went through all eight sides.

'Please bring them again, because we can't remember the words if we just hear them once,' they said, so I went away very encouraged.

One morning Leslie had just finished the daily radio communication with the missionary pilot over the two-way radio, and was listening to some of our fellow workers make their daily reports from other tribal locations. I was out on the porch giving medicine to someone, when everything began to shake. The tiles on the roof grated on each other as they moved, and the roof beams shook. We quickly ran out into the open along with everybody else in the town. We usually have several small earth tremors each year during the rainy season, but this time it was rather more severe and had lasted at least twenty seconds. The radio was still on, and soon the pilot was calling round to everybody to check if there had been any severe damage, and how extensive the quake had been. No one reported anything more severe than cracked mud-brick walls and a few tiles off the roof, but the effects had been felt as far north as Mexico City and beyond. We later learnt of severe damage on the Pacific coastal plain slightly to the north-west of our area. Everyone in Tataltepec was very stirred up about this event, and talked of nothing else for days. Very soon we had several frightened people on our porch telling us whose house had been damaged in the town, and asking us why God was angry with them, and whether this was the end of the world. We were able to tell very attentive listeners what God has to say in the Bible about the end of the world, and how those who belong to Jesus Christ do not need to be afraid.

We took turns to visit around the town to make the most of this opportunity when people were asking questions and really listening to the answers. I went to see Granny Victoria, and learnt that her house was undamaged. She had not bothered to come out during the quake because she felt that she was very old and tired, and if this was the end of the world, it was just as well, and she would be ready in her own house! However, her clay pots all lined up on the shelf were shaken off and smashed, and her pottery cups and eating bowls all rolled off the altar table to the same fate. Chona quickly offered to make new cooking pots for her mother-in-law (the cups and bowls are glazed, and must be bought at the store), but it was not the same, Granny told me sadly. These were the very ones they had used when her husband was the 'chief host' for religious fiestas, and they had held the most important feast of the year at their house. To be the 'chief host' for a year is the highest honour that a Chatino man can attain in Tataltepec, and all who have held this office are especially respected, together with their wives. No wonder Granny was sad to see her memories smashed to smithereens before her very eyes! She was not afraid, but she wanted to know 'Why?' just like everyone else. Her daughters-in-law had been terrified. Chona was full of admiration for her mother-in-law's lack of fear, and they wanted to know if we had been afraid.

Then the other woman said, 'No, I didn't think you would be after all you told us about Jesus Christ not wanting us to be so afraid. I remembered that, so I called out to Jesus Christ to save us, because you said that He is really powerful and that Most Holy Mary and the other gods and saints don't hear us when we pray to them.'

I was amazed to hear her say this, and suggested that there and then we thank Jesus Christ for listening to us, and for looking after us. This was a brand new idea to them all, but they were very happy to join in, so we thanked the Lord for looking after us all that day.

I had discovered that Granny Victoria was one of the few elderly Chatino ladies who still knew how to weave the home-spun cotton thread. She made the broad, two-yards-long white girdles that men often wear to the fields when their backs ache, and which were tightly bound round the women's waists immediately after childbirth to strengthen their backs, as custom dictated. She also made square cloths for keeping tortillas hot, which had coloured decoration and fringes. She was delighted when she heard that I would like to buy such a tortilla cloth.

'Ah yes, the old-fashioned ones made from *real* cotton keep tortillas hot much better than any of ready-made cloth from the store,' she said with satisfaction, and I readily agreed with her. She showed me her hand loom, and explained all the pieces. 'I tie the end to that cross-beam, and I thread all the "woods",' she told me, 'then I kneel on this little mat and fasten the other end round my waist to keep the cloth taut.' As always, Chona and the other nearby daughter-in-law had appeared by now, so Granny Victoria added: 'These young ones don't know how to do it, and they don't want to learn. My "woods" will just be burnt when I die, and my husband made them when we first got married.'

The younger women laughed it off, saying, 'Isn't she clever to do all that? We are much too dim-witted to learn.' So this handicraft will die out with these elderly grannies.

Some time later, I went to buy another tortilla cloth. As if on cue, Chona and the other daughter-in-law appeared as I was chatting with Granny Victoria. I chose my cloth and bought it, and then Chona said to her mother-in-law, 'Have you ever shown her your other cloth?' And then to me, 'Has the Old Lady shown you her burial dress? She has it all ready, and all the things to go with it. She made it herself some time ago.'

Granny Victoria looked a little self-conscious, and said

deprecatingly, 'Oh, she doesn't want to see that old thing!'

I assured her that I would like to see it if she was willing to show me, so she pulled a square, woven basket over towards her. It was two handle-less baskets really, one fitting tightly down on top of the other, to make a safe and private hidey-hole which no one else in the family was allowed to touch without permission. Sure enough, she lifted out of the basket a red skirt, brand new, which I duly admired. Then came a woven, white cotton over-blouse with stripes of purple ribbon to join the sections vertically, and to bind the neck. It was almost knee-length, and I stared in amazement. The women of many Mexican Indian groups wear such a huipil, though the pattern varies from area to area, and now I was seeing a Chatino one for the first time. Granny was undoing a little screw of newspaper. 'These are the beads I shall wear', she said, proffering four strands of bright red beads. 'You wear them like this,' and she tied them together round her neck with another piece of purple ribbon. 'I have shown these children how to do it,' indicating her daughters-in-law, 'and instructed them how to wrap my body properly in the over-blouse after bathing me, and putting on my new skirt. Here are the earrings too, so I am all ready.' 'But we don't want her to die yet, do we?' the daughters-in-law appealed to me, and I agreed that we did not.

Granny Victoria lived for several years more. She heard the Gospel records on various occasions, and liked what she heard. Then she caught a chest infection, and her old heart was just too tired to fight. She had said she was ready to die, but now she was rather frightened.

I don't know how much she applied to her own life of the little bit of the Gospel message that she had heard — I don't know if she really was prepared to finish her life on earth, but she died and was given an impressive funeral. Her own burial preparations were all respected, and the family kept vigil for her for nine days.

On the tenth day, great preparations were made, and a man was called in to make 'the cross and the flowers'. They gave him a small board on which he put a layer of sand. Then he asked for a small gourd each of white beans, brown beans, black beans, yellow kernels of maize, red maize and purple maize all from the family kitchens. With these he picked out a white cross in the sand, Granny Victoria's initials, her year of birth and year of death. Then he filled in the background with the various colours of corn and beans.

The altar table was made into a sort of staircase with other planks, and then covered with elaborate paper cut-outs. A woman known to be skilled in folding and cutting paper for such decorations had been called in to do this. Responsible members of the family went to everyone nearby who owned a good picture of a saint, and asked to borrow it. Then, all these pictures were arranged on the tiered altar table, with candles beside each one, and small vases of flowers. A canopy of banana leaves and palm fronds was erected over the table, and decorated with more flowers. Then 'the cross' was placed in front of the altar table, and the rest of the room was decorated and prepared for guests.

There was another all-night wake, with the town band playing slow marches hour after hour, and in the morning 'the cross' was carried in procession to the cemetery, and laid on Granny Victoria's grave, together with all the flowers that people had brought. We all mourned the passing of this old lady, because we had lost such a good friend — never again would her beaming face be seen at town functions, or looking out from her own doorway to welcome visitors.

Another friend we made about that time was Reginalda. She had often come to us for medicine for a child, or to accompany her sister-in-law or some other patient. She was always cheerful, and stayed to chat. Then one day she came and wanted medicine for herself. She was obviously much thinner, and had an irritating cough. I went through the routine list of questions, and it looked like yet another case of T.B. Besides Florida, there were five or six others on our books at this time, and both my first language helper Inés and her little son, as well as Florida's sister Macrina, had died from it. Once more I explained as clearly as I could the importance of continuing to take the medicine for a long time, perhaps a year, and the urgent need to protect the rest of the family. She agreed, and we started the routine treatment. Her condition improved rapidly, and after three months she stopped coming, as she was feeling so well, and was quite sure that she was better.

We were gone to the centre of Mitla for a while, and this time Florida had come with us. She had overcome her fear of travelling in the plane — after all, Cresenciano had returned, and he had even gone to hospital as well. The doctor confirmed our diagnosis, and ordered chest X-rays. He showed us the very definite cavity in one lung, and suggested surgery. Florida herself was horrified, and we knew that her father would never agree to such radical treatment. So we persevered with oral medicine, injections, good food and plenty of rest, and she responded. It was always a joy to have her living in the house with us, as she just assumed that she should do her share of the work — she was very conscious that we were paying her doctor's bills, but she always undervalued her own contribution to the language and translation work. Unlike Juvencio, she had no problem about catching on to the idea of hot baths for colder climates, but the doctor's order of a rest after lunch every day was her problem.

'If I lie down, I shall go to sleep, because it's so quiet here and such a comfortable bed.'

'But that's just what the doctor wants. It's good that you sleep a little in the afternoon after the morning's work.'

'Did the doctor really say, it's good to sleep in the afternoon?'

'Yes, he said that was all part of the treatment.'

'But people only sleep in the daylight if they are going to die. My grandmother would never let me sleep in the day at home, even when I was very ill. You told me to rest after dinner, but if she found me asleep, she would shake me awake again.'

So this was another reason why treatment at home of our T.B. patients was not too effective. I reiterated that it was the doctor's orders, so she obeyed, and was amazed at how much it helped.

'I'm going to tell my grandmother when I get home. It's certain that not all of the sayings handed down by our ancestors are true.'

We used the Chatino *Life of Christ* at family prayer each day, and Florida began to see its relevance and to ask a few questions. She began to take a more personal interest in the language work, and particularly in the translation.

After our return to Tataltepec, Reginalda reappeared rather sadly, and said that she had been very well for several months after her course of treatment, but perhaps we were right, and she should have continued the medicine for longer, as the symptoms were recurring. So we started again on a different course, with a strict warning that she must keep it up for many months, but once again she stopped after three months as she had improved so much she was convinced that she was cured. I still did not know where she lived, although I knew her relatives. On the other hand, Florida had really taken the doctor seriously, and was faithfully continuing to take her medicine, to the amazement of some relatives, and the ridicule of others. She seemed so well now that they could not understand it, but she had seen the 'hole' in her lung on the 'photograph' (X-ray), and was convinced that the medicine was necessary to stop the cough, so that the hole would not get any bigger.

About a year later, a small, shy man was sitting on our porch one morning. Would I come and visit his wife who was very ill?

'Has she been ill for long?'

'Yes. It just came on gradually, and now she is so thin and weak that she has to stay in bed all day.'

'Has she had any medicine?'

'Not for this illness. We kept thinking she would be better in a day or two, and then you were away, and we didn't know who to go to. She has come to you for medicine in the past, though.'

I checked through the medical bag, and went with him to 'Here Down Below'. On a steep incline near the river they had cut out a fairly level shelf, and built the family compound of three little houses on it. There were three families, and Grandad gravitated between these homes of his two sons and his nephew. All were poor, so they did not even have separate kitchens. Various relatives greeted me with shy smiles, and then I followed the sick woman's husband into the furthest house. There lay an emaciated woman under a thin blanket on the pole bed. She looked like a famine victim, and then I recognised my friend Reginalda. The T.B. was obviously rampant again, and, as I questioned her closely and took her temperature, pulse and rate of respiration, I realised that all the symptoms were very acute. I looked round the little house at the pitifully few family belongings, and understood very well why she had not continued her former courses of medicine for longer — they just had not got the money. Almost in tears I explained that I had not enough medicine to make her better there at home — perhaps if she would go to hospital they could save her life ... All the relatives had followed me in, and they listened solemnly. Her three sons were near to tears too (I later discovered that one was an orphaned nephew that she had taken in as a baby, despite her poverty, and brought up as her own). Finally her husband said:

'Well, please help her as much as you can. We don't want her to go away to hospital, because she might die there far away, and then she wouldn't be buried here in the town grave-yard. They wouldn't do it properly, because they don't know our customs, and, anyway, her spirit would never be able to find its way back home. Please give her something for the cough so that she can get some sleep, and something to stop her being sick, so that she can eat a little. Then she will be much more comfortable.'

I did what I could, and went away assuring them that I would come every day. I prayed for patience, and understanding, and wisdom, as I walked along, and I became convinced that I should really concentrate on presenting the Gospel of Jesus Christ to her.

Next day, I took the records and the little hand-operated player with me. Again the whole family was there, and even Grandad came in to hear the records. They listened eagerly, and asked questions, and wanted me to bring them again. Apparently Reginalda had slept better with the medicine I had given her, and her paroxysms of coughing did not exhaust her quite so much. I went to see her every day, sometimes with the records, sometimes I read from the *Life of Christ* and we discussed it. Once or twice Florida came with me, and we sang the few Chatino hymns and choruses, and prayed with her. Whoever was at home always came in to her house when I arrived, and listened to whatever was going on, and they all seemed interested. Reginalda told me that she was afraid to die, and asked what God's Book said about life after death. What was already translated, I read to her in answer, and other passages I explained as well as I could. She was comforted to hear of heaven.

'You say there is no more pain or sickness there? No more sadness and poverty, with not enough to eat? Play the record of "The Two Roads" again, because I want to walk on the narrow road that goes there.'

I played the record, and we prayed together. We were alone that day, and I encouraged her to talk to God too. The following day she looked quite different.

'I'm not afraid to die now. I am happy and my heart is at peace. Would you please sing that song of God about not being alone?'

So I sang, 'No, never alone', and she smiled as she followed the words. As I left, her husband followed me out, and said:

'Please bring the records again tomorrow. She isn't afraid now because she says that Jesus Christ the Boss is here with us, and she is going to where God is in charge, and there is no more pain. It says about it in God's Book, and she believes that Word.'

I arrived the next day to see my friend sitting up outside, with two women relatives holding her and dressing her. They had obviously just given her a bath, and now she was wearing her best clothes. The significance suddenly hit me as they began to do her hair, and her husband came forward to greet me with tears in his eyes. Reginalda was dead. I tried to comfort him, and told him with conviction that she was no longer in pain or suffering, but had gone to her Boss, and the wonderful place where He rules.

'Yes, she didn't cry out or anything as she died. She said she had found the narrow trail leading to God's Place, and she wasn't afraid at all because Jesus Christ was with her, and she wasn't alone. Will you come in for a few minutes? Did you bring the records? When the women have got her ready, I must go to the Town Hall to report her death so that they can ring the bell, and send the town band for the wake.'

I went in, and played the Chatino records once more while all the family listened very attentively. They discussed what they heard among themselves, and what Reginalda had said about it all. I went home convinced that now there was at least one Chatino person 'where God rules'.

10

Workshops

ONE SERVICE THAT the town desired of us in the early days was that Leslie be the town photographer. In particular, this involved taking photos of all the eighteen-year-old young men each year for their official national guard registration papers. They were required by Mexican law to march and drill in the town square every Sunday morning for a year. In rural areas this marching and drilling varied a great deal according to the capability of the local instructor, and how much school influence and discipline the youngsters have had.

One evening a town messenger appeared and said that the town president requested Leslie's presence at the Town Hall. We wondered what the summons could mean, so, following local custom, Leslie quickly put on a clean shirt and went to find out. After unhurried formal greetings, the president asked him if it would be convenient for all of that year's 'march boys' to come to have their photos taken the following day? Did we have enough black and white film? Leslie assured him that we had film, and the president asked the cost for each one. He told Leslie not to give the boys their photos until they had paid, and to keep a detailed list.

Next afternoon a light-hearted, whooping crowd of young men descended on us. We rigged up a sheet under the tamarind tree for a backcloth, and Leslie took their photos.

There were not enough uniforms to go round, so all the time they were feverishly exchanging shirts and passing the one forage cap from head to head, so that each one would look correct in his official photo. The corporal had been standing to one side, as he had been registered the preceding year and had just come as escort. He had his own uniform, and did not seem eager to mix with the crowd. He seemed rather withdrawn and stand-offish, and we afterwards found out that he was Eleuterio, commonly known as Terio. He never came to the house visiting with the other young men, and we wondered where he lived, as we never seemed to see him in the town.

One day Leslie was called to one of Florida's cousins who was very ill. Relatives gathered during his visit, and as he was about to leave, one woman said, 'Won't you come and look at my brother, please? He has been lying on his bed for months and has no strength at all. He just lives next door.'

Leslie went, and there was Terio, very pale and listless. Leslie started him on vitamins and iron and general worm medicine, but was fairly sure that he also had hookworm. Terio was not very eager to have vitamin injections, but Leslie kept going anyway. He encouraged Terio's mother to give him regular good food, but the poor woman almost wrung her hands in her anxiety, and said:

'But he won't eat it! Sometimes he gets angry with me and won't eat for a whole day to punish me. He just lies there with his face to the wall, and won't even speak to us!'

Terio was also Florida's cousin, but very unlike the rest of her lively family. Everyone said how moody he was. We saw that he would never get really better without someone firmly insisting that he regularly eat good food and take his pills.

Then we were asked to attend a translation workshop for a few months of concentrated translation work under consultant supervision. Who should go with us as a translation helper, since there were no Christians as yet in Tataltepec? We thought that this would be an opportunity to take Terio to a doctor if he would come, and to supervise his diet. So

Leslie approached his parents. If he came, he would help us put God's Word on paper in Chatino, and we would pay him a small wage, and also see that he got the right medicine. Everybody was agreeable, and so it was arranged.

There was also another young man that we were very concerned about, medically, called Nicólas. His father was a respected town elder, and had visited us on and off from our first arrival. He came for medicine for himself the first time, but always stayed to chat a little, and often brought us a little present of a coconut or something else to eat. He usually came in the evening, and was fascinated by the tape-recorder, the 'radio that speaks Chatino', and the possibility of written Chatino. One day he came in the morning and asked Leslie to go to their house as his son was ill. Leslie went with him and found that Nicolas was the patient. He was very pale, losing weight, had a fever all the time, had a persistent irritating dry cough, and a knee like a coconut. Another T.B. patient, we decided. One or the other of us went regularly to give him injections and to check up on his pill-taking, and we always enjoyed our visits to that home. They lived on top of a little hillock, and were always welcoming and gay. Nicolas lay on a straw mat in the kitchen, so that he was in the thick of all the family chats and discussions. Slowly he began to improve — the swelling on his knee went down, and he was able to bend and use his leg again.

Then we heard about the translation workshop. We immediately thought of taking Nicolas with us to see a doctor, and for him to be under more strict medical supervision, in return for helping us with the translation. He was such a likeable, attractive young man that we felt sure he would be no trouble. When we decided to take Terio as well, we approached Nicolas first, and he said that they knew each other quite well, and seemed to be very happy about the whole idea. We remembered Juvencio's loneliness with us in Mexico City, and we were glad that these two young men would be company for each other this time.

The day came when we all (that is, about a third of the population, including all of Terio's relatives and all of Nicolas's) gathered at the airstrip just at the edge of town. The little Missionary Aviation Fellowship plane came in sight, just as Nicolas's younger brother puffed up to the end of the strip with two bunches of green coconuts. One bunch was for us, and one for the pilot. Now, the plane can only take a certain weight in one load, as the airstrip is quite short and a steep mountainside rises up beyond it, so that the plane must make a sharp turn immediately after take-off. What should we do? The load was already carefully weighed, and things had been left behind so that all would fit in, and now here was twenty lb. of coconut extra, but it was a present! The pilot solved the problem by saying how hot it was, and asking to borrow someone's matchet to cut the top off one of the coconuts so that he could drink the milk. We followed suit, threw away the shells and got into the plane.

The two young men were very solemn as we took off, but were soon thoroughly enjoying their first plane flight. They tried to work out how long it would take to walk from one place to the next as the villages, rural towns and mountain ridges passed by below. Then we were landing in Mitla, and they were amazed at the dry semi-desert country there, where everything must be irrigated. They were very impressed to find that the plane had a 'house' too — the hangar seemed to them a vast size in the way of houses. The pilot's wife came out to welcome us, and invited us all to lunch.

'Yes, a bad case of hookworm, but without further complications. Just continue the treatment you planned,' said the doctor of Terio, and in just a few weeks we saw colour came back to his face, and a new vitality surge into him. The X-rays ordered by the doctor showed that Nicolas did indeed have T.B. of the lungs, but his knee was completely clear now. The doctor encouraged us to just keep up his T.B. treatment, make sure of a good balanced diet, with plenty of rest and light exercise. In contrast to Terio, Nicolas was always cheerful and cooperative, helpful in the house and thoughtful of us. He had been to school for several years, so he had a head start on Terio, and worked hard during the literacy sessions we gave them after their afternoon rest each day. He was soon able to read and write Chatino quite well. Terio had never been to school, so, day after day, he sat and looked at the page and said, 'I don't know. I can't learn because I never went to school.' We tried every kind of persuasion, and he learnt to write a tiny bit, and to read just a few words from sheer repetition, but the effort was a failure, and he was not surprised.

Various activities were arranged for the translation helpers during the workshop. The Chatino desire to conform made both fellows attend everything. So they went to the Sunday evening service, and the prayer meeting, as well as the typing class and the rambles and picnics. These joint activities were in Spanish, the national language, so the fellows wanted to learn to sing the Spanish hymns, as they did not like to be left out. Thus we started singing hymns in Spanish after the evening meal each day, but carefully explaining the words in their own language. It so happened that all the rest, from the other Mexican Indian languages represented at that workshop, were Christians. They went out of their way to be friendly to Terio and his companion, and were regularly praying for them.

Leslie was working on a panorama of the Old Testament, and I was working on the first few chapters of the Acts. Both fellows were very eager to help, and to make sure that the Chatino was clear and plain, but Nicolas seemed to respond to discussion of the meaning of a passage much more than Terio. So it happened one day, quite by accident, that Leslie was translating Exodus 32 — about Aaron making the golden calf — when I came to the parallel passage in Stephen's speech — Acts 7, 39–43. Terio was working with Leslie, and his sympathies were all with the Israelites — of course they wanted to see the god they were worshipping! He could not believe that God would really be angry about it, so he kept mistranslating some sentences. He thought that Leslie was misrepresenting God's character, and telling him, Terio, that he did not know his own language, since Leslie would not accept the mistranslation! Meanwhile Nicolas was working with me, and having the same problems. Acts 7, 42 says: 'But God turned away from them (the Israelites) and gave them over to the worship of the host of heaven . . .' The 'host of heaven' is Saint Sun, Saint Moon and all the stars, and everybody (every Chatino, that is) knows that these *are* the most important gods. So, why was I trying to say that this was God Himself's punishment? Both fellows became very upset and morose as they realised that this book that we said was God's Word did not agree with all their Chatino customs and traditions. Was it really true that the sun and the moon were neither saints nor holy? Were their old people right or not? What should they do, far from home, working with us and in our care? How could these books 'speak good Chatino' if what they said did not agree with the Chatino people?

After a very silent lunch, they went off for their doctor-prescribed afternoon rest and, in fact, we did not see them for the rest of the afternoon. An older Zapotec translation helper had particularly befriended them, so finally they went and talked it all out with him. Ciro was just the right person, because he had had a lot to do with the statues that his people worshipped before he became a Christian. He had helped to look after them, and had been in fear and awe of them, so he was able to tell the Chatino fellows that they had no power — they were just made by people's hands, so why should people worship them? He told the fellows how Jesus Christ had changed his life and how eager he was to help translate God's Word into Zapotec, so that many more of his people would know what the truth really is, and let Jesus Christ take away their terrible fears too.

The Chatino fellows had been ready to go home, but because of Ciro's friendliness they settled down again happily enough, and began to take a more positive interest in all the activities. After this crisis Nicolas was the one who took the initiative, and asked to sing to God in Chatino; it was he who was the spokesman when they wanted to learn to talk to God.

The workshop ended and they returned home much healthier than when they left three or four months previously. We hoped that they were spiritually healthy too. We followed them a month later, and as we sailed along in the small Missionary Aviation Fellowship plane we wondered what we would find. Four mountain ranges separate Tataltepec from the centre in the extra large state of Oaxaca. We came over the last range, saw a glimpse of the Pacific Ocean in the distance, and then we were descending towards the grove of coconut palms and mango trees in a small valley, which is the town of Tataltepec. We could see figures running along the trails towards the airstrip as we circled, and then we were down, with happy welcoming faces all round the little plane. Here came Nicolas, all smiles, and with a gift of green coconuts. His brother was carrying another bunch for the pilot, and he sent his greetings to the pilot's wife — he had not forgotten his first hostess. We were delighted to see him, and thought that surely he had really taken as his own testimony his favourite hymn, 'I want to follow in the steps of the Master'. We soon heard other reports though: 'Nicolas got rolling drunk the day after arriving home!' 'He does not want to work any more, just live it up with the young men and get drunk all the time.' We thought that these reports were just malicious gossip until one evening his father came to see us. Almost in tears he talked to Leslie about his son: 'He is so much better physically, and we can never thank you enough for taking him to the doctor, but please would you talk to him about this drunkenness? Surely he will soon make himself ill again if he goes on like this.'

Leslie went to their house and talked to Nicolas, but obviously he resented such interference, although he listened politely enough. He was clearly on the defensive, and after that we did not see him for several years, although the family were still our good friends.

We wondered about Terio. On the evening of our return, his parents had come to the house to welcome us back with a gift, and to tell us how well he was, and that he would soon be along to see us, when he could.

In the next few days, all our friends visited us, and gave us the latest town news and gossip. Many said, 'What happened to Terio while he was with you? He used to be so sulky and moody, and now he is always smiling and cheerful, whistling as he walks along the trail. Why, he even greeted me when I met him the other day, and he has never done such a thing before!' We began to be impatient to meet Terio himself again, but his parents had said that he was working on the family land down by the big river, three hours' walk away.

Sunday came, and as we sat down to the evening meal we were a little disappointed — it had been a restful day, but just the same as always before. Suddenly there was a greeting from the porch outside. We answered, and in bounced a beaming Terio. A word or two of welcome, then, 'It's Sunday, are we going to sing?' he asked. So we sang all that we had in Chatino — two hymns and one chorus — and then turned to the Spanish hymns he had learnt at the workshop. He had bought a hymn book and it was well used. When we were all a little hoarse, there was a pause. Then, 'Are we going to read God's Word?' he asked, and produced his copy of the Chatino *Life of Christ*, so we read. Another pause. 'Are we going to talk to our Boss?' he asked, and we prayed. It was thrilling to hear Terio pour out his heart in praise and worship to his Saviour, Lord and God, in his own language. As we listened, we began to learn how to really pray in Chatino, and we knew that God's Spirit had changed this young man so that he had become one of God's children and our brother.

Afterwards he said, 'I am at home this week. Would you have time to teach me a little if I came each evening so that I can learn to read God's Word myself?' Delightedly Leslie told him to certainly come. He came, they prayed together, and he made phenomenal progress in the reading book. He took home copies of the two Chatino hymns to practise, and was eager to help translate more hymns. He practised writing too, and in a few weeks was reading the *Life of Christ* on his own. 'I asked our Boss Jesus Christ to help me learn even if I hadn't been to school, because I wanted to read more about Him, and He did help me learn!' was the happy testimony.

The year after the workshop, Terio was on duty at the Town Hall every third week as town messenger and auxiliary policeman. This service for the town is required every second year in lieu of taxes and is performed by every man who has no other official duty. It was a real test for Terio, as the other twenty or so of his duty squad spent most of their duty hours at the Town Hall telling obscene stories and cracking dirty jokes. He found that he did not want to listen, so he moved away to sit by himself. Soon he came to ask Leslie's advice about it all, and together they looked up several New Testament passages on the subject. This gave him new strength and determination to patiently refute their jibes and to continue sitting apart during that kind of conversation, but yet remain friendly, happy and cheerful. They wanted him to drink with them too, but he steadily refused, and his good nature amazed them. Soon the lieutenant of their squad came over to sit with him, and to ask serious questions about his complete change of life and attitude. We began to hear reports of how Terio was telling people about his new Boss, Jesus Christ.

Just before we were to go on furlough, Terio again came to Leslie for advice. He was interested in getting married, so again they looked up a number of relevant New Testament passages together. He went away thinking very seriously about the matter, although he would not tell us if he had a particular young lady in mind.

It was a tremendous encouragement to us when the first letter arrived from Terio while we were in England. We thought back to those early literacy lessons at the workshop, and the failure and frustration then, which changed so miraculously after he became a Christian and wanted to know what God had to say in His book. The letter said that he was very happy following the Lord Jesus Christ, but a little bit sad because he wanted to marry, and his parents did not approve of the girl he had chosen. 'Her heart is one with my heart,' he wrote, 'and she likes me to read God's Word.' From his next letter we gathered that the difficulties with his parents had been resolved, and the third letter said that the happy young couple were expecting a baby. He still had not told us who his wife was, but tantalised us by saying that her name began with L, and she was well-known to us.

We were now very eager to return home, and to find out who this mysterious wife L was. Our arrival back in Tataltepec was a very happy day, but we had to wait some days to meet Terio and L as they were both out of town working down by the big river. Terio's parents came with a gift, welcoming as always. They were still very glad that Terio was reading God's Word and doing what it said. Yes, it was good that he had a wife now, but they did wish that he had not chosen Florencia. (We thought — Florencia? But her name begins with L? Mystery deepens!) They had wanted him to marry a fresh young girl, and to arrange it all properly, and have a three-day wedding feast with dances, in the proper Chatino tradition, but . . . We did not want to encourage their discontent on this point, so we did not probe any further. We just said, 'Well, she is Terio's wife, and he is happy, isn't he?'

'Oh yes,' responded his mother, 'they are happy, and she lookes after Terio and works hard.'

At the weekend, Terio himself came and told us that his wife was Lencha, but she was too shy to come this first time. Then we understood — Lencha is the pet name for Florencia. We had known this particular Lencha for several years, and most of her family. She had lived in a very poor little house, with her widowed mother and small sister, very close to where Terio himself lived. She was a very attractive, hard-working, cheerful girl. Too attractive in fact, so that a young well-to-do Spanish-speaker had become infatuated with her, and haunted their home. He wanted her, but he had no intention of marrying her, since there was such a gap in their social positions. All through the daylight hours he patrolled around their house for days. Then came a time when Lencha's mother was out and they needed water — finally she just picked up a water-pot and went off to the river as she saw another woman go by, telling herself that he would never molest her when she was with someone else. She thought wrong, and as she returned with the heavy water-pot, he stepped out onto the trail at a secluded spot and cut her off from her companion. The result was a little daughter, María. He took no further notice of Lencha or the child until about three years later. He was now married to someone in his own social class, and seemed very contented. So Lencha's mother thought that perhaps he was going to make some provision for María in remorse, and did not discourage his presence at their house. Once again he caught Lencha off guard.

My first introduction to Lencha and her mother was at the birth of this second baby, Claudio. Lencha was a good mother, and when the children were ill she quickly came for medical help, but, being a very poor family with few resources, their diet was very poor, and the children were continually plagued with parasites. We had been away, and when we returned, two-year-old Claudio was obviously suffering from malnutrition, helped by the many parasites distending his poor little abdomen. We treated him and his improvement was quite rapid, but no one told us of the cut that he got while out with his mother and granny one day, when they were picking coffee for someone. They washed the cut with salt water when they got home that night, and as the days passed they went on coffee picking, and it seemed to heal, but now Claudio was making no further progress physically. After a few weeks he lost his appetite, and one day he had a 'fit'. Lencha came running for help, but it proved to be a tetanus seizure, and so Claudio died.

This was why Terio's parents were unhappy — they had wanted him to marry a 'fresh, young girl', not a young woman with a child of six who had been mistreated by a superior young Spanish-speaker, and had buried yet another child! This was the girl that Terio felt was the answer to his prayer for a wife, so he had cheerfully taken on a ready-made daughter of six, and, as Lencha showed more and more interest in his Boss, the Lord Jesus Christ, Terio was satisfied. They were overjoyed when a plump little daughter was born to them the following year. She will be the very first Chatino child brought up in a Christian home. Lencha still wonders how all this new teaching fits in with Chatino custom and tradition, but she is sure that Terio is right. Terio himself is eager to see the New Testament available in Tataltepec Chatino, willing to invest a lot of time in helping with the translation, and continually praying that the Spirit of God Himself will soften and change the hearts of the Chatino people so that they will want to put God first in their lives. Occasionally he has met Nicolas. They chat amicably enough. 'But he will never talk about God's Book or about what Ciro told us at that workshop. He doesn't want to hear that Jesus Christ is stronger than the devil, and His people don't need to be afraid,' Terio told us sadly.

As our relationship with Terio had deepened, and he became Leslie's main helper with the translation, so our friendship with his cousin Florida continued, and she contributed a great deal to the translation as she worked with me daily in Tataltepec. Another time she accompanied us to the centre in Mitla. Leslie had been working at different times with Cresenciano, Taurino, and Terio on a bilingual dictionary, but now he needed to do a lot of re-organisation of the dictionary entries, and to type it all up. The head schoolteacher had promised to help him with the Spanish part of it on our return, but we needed several weeks of uninterrupted working hours for him to tackle this project.

Florida quickly slipped back into the routine of Mitla life, and was delighted to renew acquaintance with people that she had met there before — fellow Wycliffe workers, other language helpers, and the neighbours. Then came the day when she and I finished the first, rough translation of the Acts. Inevitable days and weeks of typing followed, so she took over the housework and marketing. She prepared the food and made snacks, but I still did most of the cooking, until one day I forgot the time as I typed. Florida was peeling potatoes and preparing other vegetables, I had thought, until suddenly I heard the pressure cooker. 'Well, let's see how she manages,' I thought, and went on typing. I heard the pressure come down with a hiss as cold water was poured on the cooker, then a voice said in English, 'Let's eat!' She went to call Leslie, and I went to look curiously at the table. Nothing was forgotten — she had seen that we were both busy, and it was getting late, so she had cooked an exact replica of yesterday's lunch, even to remembering that the pressure cooker needed four minutes by the clock. (She had just recently learnt to tell the time.) She had asked me no bothering questions, but just copied what she had seen me do many times. There have been many disrupted, abnormal days since, when but for Florida, there would have been no lunch until very late in the afternoon, especially when medical emergencies arise in Tataltepec.

Her very quick wit often left us floundering, as she mischieviously made puns on Chatino words to confuse us. For instance, the words 'sheet' and 'cup' differ only in the pitch of the voice, and are spelt the same. I said, 'Put the cups on the table while I make the drink,' carefully saying 'cup' on the right note, I thought. Immediately the reply came, 'Oh, but you can't put coffee on the sheets!' Straight face, twinkling eyes, and then peals of laughter at my confused look as I wondered if I had made that mistake again after all. Did I say *tasà* or *tasá*?

She was a fund of knowledge concerning family relationships in her home town, which often had us very confused, and was also our faithful adviser on local customs. Her own illness had given her lots of experience of the local curers at work, so that she could tell us their methods, and their probable reactions in other cases. She gave us an explanation of each fiesta, and how we should behave in the many strange situations in which we found ourselves involved. Her sense of humour has saved many a delicate situation, and her quickness in learning to read and write was a real encouragement to us. Some university lost a star student because Florida was born a Chatino girl in the off-the-beaten-track country town of Tataltepec.

Later on, two workshops were to be held simultaneously at the centre in Mitla. Leslie was to push ahead with the translation, while I tackled some phase of the linguistic investigation that we had not analysed very thoroughly. We took Florida and another cousin, Tito, with us. Both Terio and Florida had recommended Tito for his interest in the Christian message because of their witness, and also because he badly needed expert medical attention for his eyes. Terio himself could not come, but he seemed sure that Tito could be a real help to Leslie with the translation, and also that this method of Bible study would help Tito.

We decided that the most pressing language problem was that of the verb system. We had a list of two hundred basic verbs, with many other more complicated derivatives, but we had almost resigned ourselves to plain memorisation of these two hundred, with their past and future forms, since all but thirty seemed to be irregular, with no rhyme or reason to them. Our linguistic training had taught us that all languages have patterns, otherwise a little child could never learn his mother tongue. It's just up to the investigator to sort out these patterns, and then everything falls into place. Our experience seemed to show us that Chatino was the exception, with only thirty regular basic verbs, and one hundred and seventy irregular ones, at least! It just could not be true. So Florida and I attacked the problem, and our linguistic consultants worked with us and made various suggestions. We all prayed about it regularly. As we strictly applied linguistic procedures, a few more of those verbs fell into classes, but well over half were still irregular. Florida repeated the actual verb words hour after hour, and she thought up all kinds of little sentences illustrating their use and meaning. I made list after list of different permutations, combinations and comparisons of those basic verb words.

Meanwhile, Leslie and Tito were working hard on the Gospel of John, but they would often check out some little list of words for us, to see if they could bring any more order out of the apparent jumble of verbs. Then, one day Florida was making clear to me the difference in one verb between what occurs in English as a passive 'it is planted', and its active counterpart 'he plants'. Florida said it again, '*ntya*' — 'it is planted' and suddenly it occurred to me that the sequence of letters was very strange — what other words in the language started with nty-? I checked again with Florida to make sure.

'That's right, *ntya*. That's how you've written it each time on all the papers, isn't it?' she said, rather surprised.

She got on with preparing the next meal, while I searched through the list for other spelling anomalies. Then I searched our dictionary file for similar words that were not verbs. They did not occur. I asked Florida to think of other words beginning with nty-. We made new lists of words which began with this sequence of letters — they were all verbs! The pattern began to emerge now, in certain constructions, what ought to have been the middle of a verb word had just disappeared. We had often remarked on the fact that short words were very characteristic of the Chatino language. Now we could see how some of them had been condensed, and could even predict what a verb form would be in certain circumstances. Two hundred basic verbs became a hundred and seventy neatly classified verbs, leaving only thirty irregular ones. Now the patterns were obvious — no wonder a Chatino child of two had no problem.

11

Joy and Heartache

OCTOBER 1968 APPROACHED, and we were to leave for a year's furlough in England, so we thought we would say goodbye to everyone with a party, local style. Florida and our other friends were enthusiastic about the idea too, so they took the food preparation in hand, and another friend Malachi saw to the other arrangements, with the help of Leo and his sister. They cleared the main room of our house completely (that house had two rooms and a long porch on each side). They borrowed benches from the school to put round the walls. They set up tables all along the back porch and put more benches there. They borrowed a goodly supply of cups and plates. Then they dashed home and changed into their best clothes. They collected a couple more relatives of good social standing, and the resulting 'invitations committee' went round to almost every house in the town inviting people to the party that evening. They first got a list from us of people that *must* be included, and then invited as many more as they had time to.

Meanwhile, Florida and her food committee were busy making *tamales*, the local style meat pasties. They used two complete legs of pork, a turkey and two chickens as filling, and ground maize dough for the pastry crust. Each pasty is individually wrapped in a piece of banana leaf, and then all are steamed for several hours in a large clay cooking pot. Chona and her mother helped me with the coffee.

For entertainment Leslie had arranged for an extension from one of the stores which has a light motor to give us electricity for the evening. This would provide background music from records of our choice, and power for the little slide projector. The evening came, and so did the people. The first batch of *tamales* arrived steaming and smelling delicious, and the coffee was made. The room was decorated, and the tables were all ready, so the first relay of guests sat down and were served.

As the last guests were eating, Leslie hung a sheet on the outside wall of the house for a screen. By now four hundred or so people had arrived, so they could not possibly all squeeze into that one room. Leslie showed the slides that they like best — the ones of themselves and their own town and activities — and everyone was delighted.

We were gone for the year, and one of the great events during that time was the arrival of letters from both Terio and Florida. We were saddened to hear of all the deaths that they told us about, especially of Florida's young brother, but we were thrilled by the tangible evidence of this correspondence that these two now really understood about communication by means of words on paper.

Then we were back, and there was so much to catch up on. People seemed glad to see us, although many had not believed that we would return at all. Soon after our arrival, came the boxes of new books — the book of Old Testament Bible stories, started at that first translation workshop with Nicolas and Terio, was at last in print. Some of the young men who had begun to understand what we were doing had said that they wanted a fat book, to show that there were real books in Chatino. Now, here was this impressive, fat book, with the attractive yellow cover. Terio was one of the first to see it, and it was so encouraging to see him just sit down immediately and start studying it.

Taurino borrowed one to read at home, and later came back with a smile. 'Now this really speaks Chatino. No one can say they don't know anything about God if they read this.'

Christmas was near, when a woman asked me to go and see her daughter who was very ill. This girl, Chica, was an old friend with a very sad history. Another cousin of Leo's, she and her brother had lost their father when they were quite small. Their mother had married again — a widower with three little sons of his own — and each of the partners seemed determined to prove to the other that the children they had brought to this new family partnership would be no burden or hindrance. As new little brothers and sisters were born, these five older ones got more and more work to do, and less and less to eat. Chica learnt to do the entire family wash at a very early age, and soon took over most of the cooking as well, while her mother went out to work in the field alongside her husband. Chica and her brother had inherited a small coffee plantation from their dead father, but their mother administered this, and put the income into the family coffers.

At fourteen, Chica first came to us for medical treatment, with liver trouble. We suspected an abscess and treated her accordingly. This diagnosis was confirmed by a doctor two or three months later. When she recovered, she felt better than she had ever done, because of the vitamins that we had needed to administer. Then she got engaged to Cresenciano's brother — her second cousin. They were head-over-heels in love, and her mother and step-father were relieved to see her arranged for so creditably. Cresenciano's family all liked her, so there was no hindrance to the marriage. They observed all the Chatino traditions, but no one knew when the priest would come to town again to perform any church weddings, so it was decided that she should move in with her fiancé's family anyway, and the church ceremony would just be a matter of form when the priest eventually arrived. Everyone was happy with this arrangement, and, in a week or two, Chica was looking better physically, as she was eating so much better and, while busy, was not overworked.

She blossomed out as an attractive, cheerful and industrious fifteen-year-old.

Then the priest came, and Chica's young husband was one of the first to go to the Town Hall to pay the fee and get his credentials. He took this 'ticket' to the priest, with his request for marriage.

'But aren't you two cousins? I can't marry cousins!' he was told. Perhaps if he had been able to explain the relationship better in Spanish, or had had someone influential to plead his case, the result would have been different. The young man was completely bowled over by this refusal, and by the time he got home he was furious and bitter. He threw down his 'ticket', and said:

'Well, the priest won't marry us. He says we can't be married, ever, so I'm going away.'

Nothing could dissuade the disillusioned young man, and, without a word to his beloved Chica, he left home and was not heard of again for several months. His parents became quite worried about him, and it also became apparent that Chica was pregnant. Once, the young man returned to a relative's house at the edge of town and sent a message to his father. When he learnt that Chica was still in their house, he would come no nearer home, but after talking to his father, left the town again for several more months. His father had told him that he was to have a child, but he refused to own it, or to hear Chica mentioned. When Chica heard this report, she sadly said goodbye to his family, thinking that it would be better for everyone if she went back to her mother, even though it was in disgrace, and with the same old family drudgery awaiting her.

Her liver began to play up again, and I was called in once more. Then I was on hand for the birth of her baby daughter. Her uncle, Leo's father, was there to support her if necessary, since she had neither husband nor father. I was glad that the birth of little Lydia was easy on her young mother.

Everything went well until Chica's mother had a new baby, and then Chica and Lydia were constantly reminded that they were 'orphans' and only tolerated by kind, long-suffering relatives. Chica worked harder than ever as the family slave, and did other people's washing as well, to earn a little money to buy clothes for herself and Lydia. Now Lydia was nearly two-and-a-half years old, and Chica had been very ill for weeks, so no one had looked after the child, and she was dreadfully undernourished and full of intestinal parasites.

I followed Chica's mother to the house, and was appalled at what I saw. The girl was all puffy with oedema. She was still sitting up, but it was obvious that only sheer will-power kept her upright. I knew nothing about heart trouble, but when I felt Chica's pulse jumping and jerking erratically, I knew there must be something wrong with the heart. They gave me very vague answers to most of my questions, and I could not seem to build up a medical picture that corresponded with her condition. I went home and searched the books, and then asked for medical advice on the radio. I had started giving Lydia worm medicine and vitamins, but I had heard her cough, and I was afraid she had tuberculosis.

At the same time, Leslie had his emergency too — a lad of seventeen on the other side of the town, also fatherless. However, both his mother and his step-father (who turned out to be another uncle of Chica's) seemed to be considerably more concerned about him than anyone was about Chica. This Lario had been having terrible headaches and a high fever, and now was partially paralysed all down his right side.

Christmas passed, and our patients were no better, perhaps a little worse. We asked for more advice, but we made no headway. Florida was not too well either. As we prayed about it, we both felt that we should take them all out to the doctor. In Mitla we could at least give them proper care, and still get a little desk-work done. If their parents would show good faith by producing a minimal contribution to the cost, we would take them. The next morning, Lario's step-father asked if it would be possible to get him to a doctor, and so

Leslie made his proposition. They produced the money almost immediately, and we felt that this was good corroboration. Then I approached Chica's family.

'Oh yes, we would like her to go,' said her mother, 'but you must remember that she's a poor orphan with an orphan child abandoned by its father. I don't know how she could raise that money.'

Chica had whispered to me only a few minutes before:

'Don't worry about the money — my mother has money because she sold a whole sack of our coffee just yesterday, and there is another one in the corner. It really belongs to my brother and I, but she wants to use the money for the little children.'

With this in mind, I asked her mother:

'Do you think she will get better here? What about Lydia? Do you want to watch them die? Two funerals would be very expensive here where all the customs must be followed. I can't help them any more because I don't know enough, but a doctor could help them. Yes, it's true that they might still die in Mitla, but at least we will have done all that we could. Left here they will certainly die.'

'Well, I'll see if I can find a buyer for some of my coffee, but they are paying a very low price at the moment, so it won't be easy. I'll tell you tomorrow.'

I went home feeling rather defeated, and we put the proposition to Florida anyway.

'I would like to come and help you. Yes, I would like to see the doctor again. Do you think I could ever really get better? I would like to help look after Chica, because her mother has been very unkind to her. Everyone knows that she is not poor really.'

We asked the pilot to stand by in the next day or two for an emergency medical flight, and we continued desperately to ask for God's help in the situation.

The next day Chica's mother had just sent a child out to sell some coffee beans when I arrived. The child returned with the money.

'Look, I've got eighty per cent of what you said. Will you take coffee beans for the rest?'

Wearily I agreed, wondering what would ever convince this woman that I was not trying to cheat her, that this money was not even enough to pay the M.A.F. fare and the first visit to the doctor, let alone cover the subsequent expenses. I urged them to be ready the next morning, and to arrange for relatives to carry the hammock to the airstrip. Then I ran home with the news. Leslie immediately went to inform the other family.

We packed up the house again, and informed our friends.

'But when will you come back?'

'When the sick ones are better,' we replied.

There was not room in the little plane for everyone, so Leslie was to go by land, and would see us in a couple of days. He would start out early the next morning. So, on the day of the flight, representatives from all three families were on hand at radio time, and, as soon as the pilot said he was taking off from Mitla, the message went to Florida to come right away, and to Lario's and Chica's families, to carry their patients out to the airstrip. The flight takes just over forty minutes, so we scurried round to dismantle the radio, close up the house and get ourselves out to the airstrip in time. It seemed as if the whole town had gathered there to see us all off, and we assured the parents that we would write and tell them of their children's progress.

The pilot expertly packed us all in, and then we were airborne. It was a great relief to actually be on the way, and I could not help praising God for His mercy and help. In Mitla our fellow workers already knew of the emergency; the pilot had told everyone about our radio messages, so they had been praying especially for us, and were only too willing to help us when we arrived. Two men whisked us all straight to the doctor's surgery, where he attended to us immediately, ahead of the queue in his waiting room. Then we went on into the town to the house where we were to stay and set up our Chatino mini-hospital for a little while.

Several friends dropped in to help me get organised, and Florida went out to buy some supplies. I realised again just how much we rely on the rest of the team, as people working there at the centre helped us, and other translation personnel came in to enquire how things were. Fellow workers' children came to play with Lydia.

'We were praying for your Chatino sick people at school today,' one told me. Another brought a little bundle with:

'My mummy said, would these clothes be any use to the little girl, because my baby sister has outgrown them.' Someone else brought us a cake. 'I didn't suppose you would have time to bake,' she said.

Chica and Lario were amazed at people's kindness and thoughtfulness. They asked Florida about it, as they knew she had been with us to Mitla before.

'Are they all related then? Do they all come from the other side of the sea?'

'Oh no, but they are all People of Jesus Christ (Christians). That's why they are interested and concerned.'

Leslie arrived after a couple of days, and we began the real hospital regimen. We had divided up the big bedroom so that Chica and Lydia had a bed at one end, we were in the middle, and Lario was at the other end. Florida slept on a camp bed in the study, as she had before. Both Lario and Chica needed doses of medicine in the middle of the night, and little Lydia needed attention that her mother could not give. Lario's capsules were enormous, and he was sure that he could not swallow them with just water. So Leslie made him coffee for his midnight dose, which solved that problem — except that we had no thermos; but cold coffee did not seem strange to Lario.

That same day, Chica seemed to have difficulty breathing sometimes, but we knew that it was the doctor's day off, and he was out hunting. His competent wife, a nursing midwife, stood in for him, but we did not want to call her unless it was absolutely necessary. In the early evening Chica suddenly cried out and had a convulsion, so Leslie borrowed a bike and rushed up to the doctor's house. We followed the instructions, but there was no improvement, and we could not feel her pulse. So, leaving a message for her husband, the doctor's wife left her own children to their meal, and came down to help us. Florida took charge of Lario and Lydia, fed them and made them a bed in the kitchen. Chica's convulsions continued, and the three of us held her and just watched in helpless desperation. Then we heard a motor-bike, and the doctor himself rushed in and took over. He still had deer's blood on his trousers, as he had not stopped to change when he saw his wife's note. It was heart failure, and as soon as Chica began to calm down — as a result of his attention — he pointed out the symptoms, and told us exactly what he had done, and why, so that we would know again in a similar emergency. The doctor and his wife finally left us at midnight.

'Let me know first thing in the morning if she is still alive, Leslie, and I'll be down. The next few hours are the crucial time, but you two must take it in turns to get some sleep.'

By dawn she had got rid of quarts of fluid, and the swelling was visibly reduced. Her pulse was feeble, but it was there. Then she woke up:

'Was I very ill last night, Old Lady? Suddenly everything went black, and I was fighting to breathe. Then I screamed, and I don't remember any more, except that I'm sure you and the Old Man were here with me. Did the doctor come?'

I explained as much as I could to her, and Leslie went to report progress to the doctor, while I reassured the rest of our household. The doctor came, and gave her a thorough examination.

'She must have had rheumatic fever, and now she's got rheumatic heart disease,' he told me. 'Her heart is terribly damaged, and only one valve is working. She can't live like that! It's a medical impossibility.'

'Well, she has come out of the heart failure.'

'Yes, and we will do everything that we can without a hospital intensive care unit and a whole battery of tests, but it needs a miracle to save her.'

'God still does miracles,' I reminded him, 'and we shall all be praying for that miracle.'

He gave me an odd look, and said that he would be back the next day. He glanced at Lydia with a smile as he left. She was sitting on a mat in the sun holding a little plastic bear, and staring at it solemnly. She soon got to know him because of his daily visits, and would often follow him in to see her mother, where he would take her up on his knee and talk to her. At two-and-a-half, she weighed only fourteen-and-a-half pounds on the day we flew in to Mitla. When the doctor first saw her, he flew into a rage, and I was glad Chica's mother was not nearby as he stormed up and down his surgery thundering in Spanish and English about the ghastly results of ignorance and neglect. Lydia had just stared at him solemnly, with big unblinking eyes — somehow she knew that he was not angry with any of us present, and she was not afraid. The nurse and his wife came running in at all the commotion, and were ordered out without an explanation. The patients in the waiting room shook in their sandals to hear the tirade.

'What that child needs is food. Basically there is nothing wrong with her except a few intestinal worms, but she looks like a famine victim, with only a week to live.'

He had given us medicine and food supplements for her, and already she had a healthy appetite. Daily she grew stronger and took more interest in what was going on.

Lario too was improving. We had to bully him into exercising his affected leg and arm, as he had got so used to them being almost useless. But the doctor had said he was to walk a little further each day, so we persevered, and gradually he forgot to use his stick.

The doctor came every day for three weeks, and he filled as much of his prescriptions as possible with sample medicines and extras to help us. He charged for none of this, but the other medicines had to be bought at the chemist's. He prescribed for Florida once more, and said that her biggest need was rest and good food, although he wanted a new chest X-ray for comparison. On the Saturday he took me on one side and said:

'You know, you must be prepared. Chica could go at any moment. Her heart has not improved, and there is no medical reason for her to still be alive at all. No one can live with only one valve working in their heart. You people had better start praying!'

'Why do you think she is still alive?' I countered.

'There is certainly no medical reason, so it must be a miracle, but she needs a bigger one to *stay* alive. You have been in a constant state of emergency for a long time now, and I know it is hard, but you *must* be prepared for her death at any time. I'll be back tomorrow.'

I went slowly back indoors. Yes, we had got used to her condition, and I was jolted by his words. But God must have a plan for her, or surely she would have died when her heart failed three weeks before, or at home when she first had the rheumatic fever? She herself was sure that she was much better, and was convinced that God had done a miracle in her body. She had thanked Him gratefully, and daily wanted to learn more about Him, and about what Jesus Christ had done. She eagerly listened to the Gospel records and to any Scripture that we read with her, and asked questions of both Florida and myself. She wanted to learn to sing and to read when she was a little stronger — but would she get stronger? Leslie and I talked over the doctor's words and prayed together, and then we told the news to any of our fellow workers that passed by. All that weekend they prayed in families and little groups, and on Monday the schoolchildren prayed again.

On Tuesday the doctor examined Chica as usual, then he frowned, and went through his routine again. Then he said to me:

'Well, I can't understand it, but that heart is better. Two valves are working, and a third is trying. It's a miracle.'

'You told us to pray, Doctor.'

'Well, I have to admit that God listened, but she's got a long way to go yet.'

His visits became less frequent then, but obviously Chica's convalescence would be slow. He had discharged Lario, so Leslie decided to take him home, and to stay out in Tataltepec alone for a month, as we had been there such a short time after our year's absence. Florida's health was improving by leaps and bounds, so perhaps she could return home when Leslie came back, and so make good use of the plane.

While Leslie was away, two or three of the Wycliffe men called round regularly to see if there was anything that needed their help. We carried Chica's bed outside into the garden for several hours each day, so that she felt more a part of everything. Florida would bring the vegetables out so that she could help in their preparation, and she began to learn to read. We all did jig-saws together, and she was able to watch Lydia for an hour or so while Florida and I worked at the desk. We started to translate the letters to the Thessalonians, and Florida was fascinated by the references to the return of Jesus Christ to earth, and the state of dead Christians. We discussed this a little, and some of the parallel passages. Suddenly the implications of the resurrection hit her, and she burst out 'You mean, I shall get a new body like our Boss (Jesus Christ) did? You mean that I won't have to live for ever with this horrible, old, thin, sick body, but He will give me a new one, so that I can really thank Him and make Him big (praise Him)? Then it's true that we will be really happy with Him in His place? I'm really looking forward to it.'

She told Chica all about this new bit of God's Word, and obviously it was thrilling news to them both. It was an encouragement to all our friends as I quoted the girls' reactions.

Everyone took notice of Lydia. The men who called in would pick her up, and throw her up in the air, and Chica loved to see them playing with her. Lydia became so accustomed to this attention that, when one of them walked in, she would come up to him holding her arms up ready to be picked up. Suddenly, one day, we became aware of her chortling with delight as she was thrown into the air and caught again. Chica looked up and said to me:

'That is the first time in her life that she has ever laughed. She has never spoken a word, and never laughed before, and she very seldom cried.'

Lydia still found plenty of ingenious ways to communicate without uttering a word, but she did lots of laughing from that day on, and occasionally cried pathetically. The next time the doctor saw her, he said with satisfaction:

'Ah, now I have a child on my knee, not a warmed up corpse.'

The pilot came to tell us that Leslie had arranged a flight for the next day, and if Florida was ready at eight a.m., he would pick her up and take her to the airstrip. So she went home, and Leslie returned, and we settled into a new routine. Chica was up and about a little now, so she insisted on helping in the kitchen. She was also eager for her daily lessons in reading and writing, and began to look forward to little outings when people invited us for a ride in a car. The doctor said she was to walk a little further each day, so we began to visit people that had called in to see her. It was a great day when we walked all the way up to the doctor's for her check-up — about a mile — and we began to think about our return to Tataltepec. Chica and Lydia had been in Mitla four months, and in that time Lydia had gone through three sizes of shoes, grown two inches, and now weighed twenty-seven-and-a-half pounds.

Leslie's month-long stay in Tataltepec had been quite difficult as he coped with callers and medical cases, and cooked his own meals. People had been very helpful and understanding though, and he had had plenty of varied language practice. However, he had come back to Mitla with one very critical item of news. The house we were renting had been sold and the new owners needed it. We had paid our rent till the end of the year, and they were quite happy about that, but in the new year we would have to move. So, now what? Lord, you sent us to Tataltepec, and we haven't finished the translation or anything else, but You know that there is no other house available . . .

We thought of the whole Chatino area — still there was no news of any other team coming to tackle the other languages. We thought of all those copies of the Gospel of Mark in the Yaitepec language. A Gospel Recordings' technician had taken a pile and sold some, when he was in that area once, but otherwise they had never been distributed, and no more had been done. Perhaps we should move to Juquila, the county town, and have a Tataltepec family stay with us for several weeks at the time, so that one of us could continue work in the Tataltepec language, and the other one re-learn the Yaitepec language? Our Director appeared on the scene at about this time, and discussed the whole matter with us:

'Haven't you considered building in Tataltepec? I tend to favour the idea of your finishing your task there first.'

'But we don't really believe in owning property in this job,' we told him. 'We are afraid that our roots will go too deep, and we won't want to move when it really is time to move.'

'Yes, property can be a tie, but have you considered that perhaps the Lord wants you to have a better and more efficient living situation? You certainly didn't enjoy the very best of conditions when I visited you there in the centre of town with just the one big room, and all those loudspeakers blaring in your ears. I know this other house has been a bit better, but that is no longer available. Don't entirely rule out the possibility of building. Let's pray about it.'

Did God really want us to build a house? We could not believe it, but since the Director had said to consider it seriously, we thought that we should make a list of all the factors that would point towards building, and all the desirable improvements on our present circumstances that we would like to see in a new house.

Before leaving Mitla we had letters from more than one respected Christian friend to say that they thought we should build a house, and even sending gifts towards the construction. From the church they wrote to say that the Sunday School had already started saving for our new house.

People welcomed us back as usual, and everyone was amazed to see Chica and Lydia so healthy. Apparently, many people had never expected to see either of them again. In the evening Leslie made a formal visit to the Town Hall to report our return. He also mentioned that our house had been sold, so we could not live there any more, and he asked permission to build a house.

'Where do you want to build?' was their reaction. Leslie then told them that we had wondered if we would have to leave altogether, but if they were happy for us to build in their town, perhaps they would tell us the sites available.

'You go out and choose the place where you would like to build a house, and then let us know so that we can register it for you. You will really be a part of this town if you build a home here,' they told him. Again things were moving faster than we were. If it was up to us to choose a site, then we had certain pointers in mind, so Leslie explored the edge of the town out towards the airstrip. On Sunday we went for a walk together, and he showed me a place, in the shade of a wild fig tree, which gently sloped down to the airstrip itself. There were some big rocks at the top, and mountains all round. A little hillock cut out noise from the centre of the town, and the only domestic animals in sight were donkeys tethered on the airstrip. The main trail to Juquila went past about twenty yards away, and the work trail to the town brick and tile works crossed the airstrip on the other side of the fig tree. It would be a marvellous site for a house. We sat on the big rock and worshipped God as we revelled in the quietness and peace, and in the beauty of His creation surrounding us.

When Leslie rather diffidently told the Town Council of this site, they asked:

'Have you put up a fence round it?'

'I thought you wanted to check it over first.'

'Oh no. There is plenty of space out there by the airstrip. Just clear the patch you want and put a fence round it, then we will come and see it, and enter it in the records.'

We were flabbergasted — it was all so easy, and we were just about convinced.

But now the thing that had always worried us (apart from ownership) came to the fore. How could we spend months and months just on building a place to live, when language work and translation was crying out to be done? At least we had a deadline — we had to move in at the New Year, and it was now May. From the end of May there would be five months of the rainy season, but God seemed to have everything planned, so Project Housebuilding began.

PART THREE

'New' Tataltepec

12

Housebuilding

TAURINO WAS CONVALESCING again. He thought he could manage to clear the land and help to put up the fence. Lario's step-father had a few tiles to sell to go on the roof. Several men were willing to help with digging for water, including Chona's husband Delfino and his cousin Marcelo. People on their way to or from their fields began to stop regularly to enquire how the hole was going. As the digger disappeared, and a pulley was set up to get out the bucket-loads of earth, the question everybody asked was:

'Will you find water there? How do you know?'

We did not know for sure, but we had good reason for expecting water at that spot. Soon, most of the men were afraid to dig at the bottom of the hole because it was so deep, but Marcelo persisted. Delfino told us apologetically:

'I want to help, and I'll pull up bucket-loads of earth all day, however heavy they are, but I just can't stand to be in that tiny space underground.' Several others agreed with him.

Five metres deep — no water. Ten metres deep — no water. No one in Tataltepec had ever dug so deep, and many were convinced that there was no point in continuing. When Marcelo was not available, Leslie dug at the bottom of the hole. They had come to a layer of rock and the going was very slow at this point. The rains began, and they had to stop and build a roof over the top, but then they could not see at the bottom of the hole, so Marcelo took a candle down, made a niche in the wall for a sardine-tin to stand it in, and the work went on. At eleven metres things began to get quite wet; by twelve metres they had clearly found water, but the base was very hard to chip away. So when they had a steady flow of water at twelve-and-a-half metres, they stopped. They cleaned it up, and Leslie built a top for the well hole, and then people started asking for a drink as they passed. The men pronounced it good drinking water, and so water was found on the site.

Now for the foundations. We got out our plan, and Leslie went to see a young Chatino mason. Yes, he thought he could do it, even in the rainy season, and he would get his own workmen, if Leslie would give him the contract and pay an all-in figure. Leslie would arrange for the materials — rocks, lime, a little cement — and the job would be completed by the end of August. It turned out that Florida's father was a lime burner, so he provided the lime, and there were plenty of rocks at the site which just needed to be broken up. The mason and his gang almost gave up one week when torrential rain kept them from working at all. They covered what they had done with plastic sheeting, and made gloomy forecasts about their work. Then, as usual, the rain lessened during August, and they triumphantly finished the job. The mason came to report completion in the evening, and asked if Leslie would go and inspect the work with him the next morning, and would he please take his camera. In the morning a very spruce mason in his best clothes arrived to escort Leslie to the scene. His gang of three assistants (all old friends of ours) joined them on the way, equally dressed up for the occasion. They arranged themselves, with their tools, standing on the foundations for the photos, and were all delighted when they received their colour prints later on.

At the end of August, we went to Mexico City for the biennial conference of the Mexican Branch of Wycliffe. It was good to hear reports from all the other translation teams and from the centres, and everyone wanted to know how our housebuilding was going. News of complete New Testaments translated is always encouraging, and the reports of people reading translated Scripture for themselves, and of God speaking to them through it, moved all our hearts. His Church does consist of believers from every people and tongue, every tribe and nation, and as we glimpsed a little of His proof of this, we were amazed and praised Him together.

Back at Mitla we consulted with the M.A.F. builder, Claire, and his wife, Arlene. What construction materials did we need that were not available locally? When did the rainy season usually end? We had decided on rammed earth for the walls, as Claire had adapted this original French technique for use in rural Mexico. Rammed-earth houses appear very similar to the customary mud-brick house, but are much quicker and cheaper to build. Claire said that he would make the moulds for this, and bring the tamping irons. Arlene was quite excited, because Claire had been involved in several building projects in different villages, but she had not been able to go with him before, as the children had been at home. Now, at fifteen, their youngest had joined his brother at boarding school, as our little Wycliffe school in Mitla only catered for children up to that age.

Metal doors and windows were being welded in Mitla, and we had acquired a number of glass bricks to let in more light. Back in Tataltepec, Leslie arranged for sand and gravel to be carried from the river, lime to be burnt, rafters to be cut, slats to be split, tiles to be made to lay on them, and the main ridge pole to be felled and brought in to hold up all the rest of the roof. Our friends rallied round, and Cresenciano and others guided animals loaded with sand and gravel to and from the river; Terio's father and Florida's father burnt lime, and brought it; Nicolas's father cut rafters; Juvencio split oak slats; Lario's step-father, Florida's uncle, and others made tiles; another of Florida's uncles, who trains yokes of oxen, felled appropriate trees out on the mountain-side, to be used for the ridge pole, and then the current oxen-in-training dragged them down to the site.

In mid-November Claire and Arlene arrived. Somehow, the pilot had contrived to pack the windows and doors in as well, and all Claire's bit and pieces. Florida and Chica were on hand to welcome Arlene, who had always been very friendly to them in Mitla. Now the work began in earnest as six to ten men worked with Claire and Leslie each day to dig earth out of a hole, pour it into a box-like mould, tamp it down firmly, and move on to the next one. They found that the top soil was too crumbly, and the best earth was just plain sub-soil. No water was added, because it was damp enough already. They soon got into a routine, and Arlene and I would carry out a big pot of lemonade in the late afternoon for a little break. They had lots of visitors, and every passer-by was curious to see how they were doing this building with just earth.

By December 20th, the windows and doors were all in, and the walls were almost finished. Taurino had painted all the windows and doors, and had assisted the mason who fitted them and made the concrete sills. Regretfully, we saw Claire and Arlene return to Mitla, as several of their children were to come home for Christmas. Leslie and Taurino were able to set up and take down the moulds now, and quite a lot of men had learnt this new method of construction, so Claire was assured that they could complete the job without him.

By New Year's Day, it was all done except the roof, but all the materials for that were on hand, including the ridge-pole — in three sections. The younger boys' Bible class at our home church had wanted to help with a special project to do with the house, so they had provided that ridge-pole. When we wrote to thank them, we told them:

> 'You can't have a house without a ridge-pole, because that's what keeps the whole roof up; so it really is the most important part.'

Now Leslie's immediate problem was, how to get that 'most important part' up into its place, so that it could function. The poles looked enormous as they lay there on the ground, and men kept trying the weight of one end and shaking their heads. For the last few days our friends had been hinting:

'You are going to have a proper roof-raising to finish the house, aren't you? We'll come and help.'

Finally we were persuaded that they really meant it, but the ridge-pole would have to be in place the day before. A picked gang of men helped Leslie to manhandle those great logs into place, and lock them together, and our friends were all alerted that the next day, January 5th, the roof would go up. Meanwhile, Florida, Chona and Taurino's wife were organising the food. Chona's family shucked the corn, and we put it on to boil. Taurino's family helped us pick over the black beans and wash them. Then we put them to soak overnight so that they would cook faster.

The next day, men gathered on our porch right after breakfast, and others went straight out to the house. Those who owned useful tools, such as hammers and saws, took them, and everyone took his matchet. Soon after they had gone, their women-folk began to gather with kitchen buckets and plastic bowls. They decided who would work in Chona's kitchen, and who with Taurino's wife; then each one took some of the cooked maize in her receptacle. Balancing the bowls and buckets on their heads, they formed two lines behind their leaders who, with money in hand for the corn-mill, led their assistants off in two long lines to get the maize ground. Florida and I had the beans bubbling in a big pot over an open fire on the back porch, but soon we heard the motor start up for the mill, and not long after we saw one line of women returning to Taurino's kitchen next door to pat out and cook the tortillas.

The beans were all right, so we started another fire for the coffee pot. Then we considered the matter of seating and serving. We borrowed tables from our Spanish-speaking neighbours to augment our own, and increased the seating by using spare planks between the chairs. Malachi's family came to the rescue again with extra bowls and cups, and Florida made some hot chile pepper sauce. We put small containers of salt and of chile sauce down the middle of the tables, and then the hot tortillas began to arrive in piles. They were wrapped in a cloth inside a basket, so that they would stay fresh and hot. The younger women stayed to help serve, and someone called out from the front porch, 'Here they come,' so we started ladling out beans into the bowls. When the men had finished and returned to work, we washed the bowls quickly, and ladled out a bowlful of beans with two tortillas on top for each woman who had helped. They took this home, and finally Florida and I sat down to eat our own meal.

Then we cleared up, and made a great pot of lemonade. I took this and went to see the progress on our new house. They were laying the tiles now, and it looked marvellous. A few men came back next morning to finish up, and Leslie started to lay a thin plaster on the outside of the walls, to stop the bees and other insects from burrowing in. And so we moved in. Concrete floors, plaster on the inside walls, shower, sinks, porches outside, all came later, but we were very glad to be in our own convenient house.

Chona came herself with the tortillas to inspect the new house.

'Rodrigo came out here to see his father at work when they were doing the roof,' she told me — he was now about four years old — 'and at supper that night he had us all laughing. "We live in Old Tataltepec," he said. "The Old Man is building his house out there by the airstrip in New Tataltepec. I want to move out to New Tataltepec, Dad. Can we go and choose a site there tomorrow?"'

'So we few families who have houses out here by the air-strip are living in New Tataltepec, according to Rodrigo?' I answered. 'When are you going to leave Old Tataltepec to join us?'

'When Rodrigo has persuaded his father, I expect. He offered to go out and help him cut the main corner posts and the ridge-pole, ready for our new house!'

'Your little boy is growing up, Chona. He thinks for himself.'

The front door led into the clinic — the biggest room in the house, and we put up a temporary porch of plastic sheeting and coconut fronds out there for people waiting for medicine. The back door led into the general reception room — the next biggest room — and we put the alphabet frieze up round the wall, just to catch people's attention, and to illustrate some Chatino words.

We soon found that we had less visitors now, but people came who really wanted to talk. One was the late Reginalda's son, Gabino, a very shy fellow who wanted to hear the records and to talk about Jesus Christ. He wanted to learn to sing, too. He said that he had always remembered the records from when I played them for his mother, and he had thought a lot about what she had said before she died — how she believed in Jesus Christ and wanted to follow His road, and go to where He rules, and be with Him for ever. He told us that, many Sunday evenings, he had followed Terio to our house in the past, and stood outside in the darkness listening to us sing 'the songs of God'. He had been too shy to come into the house there in town, but now he wanted to learn to read more, to hear more of God's Word, to talk to God and to sing hymns.

14

Those 'Other Chatinos'

WHEN WE CAME to Tataltepec, we had wondered:

'Is it right to establish ourselves in the Chatino language spoken by the smallest number of speakers, when the other Chatino languages are spoken by so many more people?'

From surveys of the Chatino area that Leslie had conducted we knew that there were four distinct languages — two spoken by the people living in the mountains, the language spoken in and around Zenzontepec and Tataltepec Chatino.

Yet God had clearly brought us to Tataltepec and we were becoming increasingly aware of how strategically the town was situated. People from the nearer mountain area came down to buy cattle, pigs and maize, while people from the Zenzontepec area came through on their way to other places, or to sell coffee.

With a great effort we can cast our minds back to Yaitepec days, and manage to converse, rather haltingly, with the mountain people. They are very patient and understanding and, by taking time, we manage to communicate. From time to time old friends from Yaitepec itself have stayed the night with us, and have enjoyed listening to the Gospel records in their language.

It is a different matter with the people from the Zenzontepec area. Through the years we have learnt a little medical vocabulary in their language, but nothing else. Usually they make sure to come with one of their neighbours who speaks a little Spanish, so that they can communicate with the shopkeepers, but often the Spanish dries up when it comes to describing medical symptoms. We have learnt to send for Simón if we are in real difficulty.

Simón came to Tataltepec as an orphan child of less than ten-years-old, and was kindly taken in by one of the richer, Spanish-speaking families. He came from the collection of hamlets that makes up Santa María, and he still has several relatives there. He did various odd jobs and errands in gratitude for his keep, and soon learnt to speak Spanish, as he had no other means of communication. He did not forget his own language, as his relatives and friends of the family always called in to see him when they came to Tataltepec for any reason. Simón is of a friendly, gregarious disposition, but he was a very lonely little boy, as the children of his benefactors only accepted him on sufferance, knowing him to be a 'charity child'. They laughed at his mistakes as he tried to speak Spanish, and made him the object of their teasing. The local Chatino children did not accept him either, because they could not understand what he said when he spoke the Zenzontepec Chatino language, and he did not understand them. So they too laughed at him.

It must have dawned on this unfortunate child that the only acceptable thing in his situation was to be someone worth laughing at — or perhaps this was his subconscious reaction. Anyway, he became a very entertaining clown, and people have continued to enjoy his antics ever since. So he made his own place on the Tataltepec scene, and was accepted on those terms.

As he grew up, he became a muleteer, and worked for the owners of the general stores, regularly bringing their mule trains of supplies for the shops from El Paso, or even from Jamiltepec. He would take any bulk cargo that they had to sell to the outside world, like maize, hot chile peppers or coffee beans. A responsible member of the family would go too, to see to the sale of such goods, and the ordering of further supplies. From these trips, he became very well known in El Paso, and in course of time he got engaged to a girl from there. She was a Spanish-speaker, but like Simón, was an orphan with few close relatives, and so, very poor.

His benefactors helped him pay for a modest wedding, and he brought his bride to the tiny home that he had built not far from the big, substantial houses of his benefactors and employers. In spite of their poverty they always throw open their home to anyone from Santa María with any claim at all on Simón. Simón's wife does not enjoy very good health, probably because of malnutrition as a child, and continuing poverty now, and never has enough milk to feed her babies. We made their acquaintance during our first year in Tataltepec, when they were feeding the baby cornflour gruel, often without milk, and they wondered why it was so tiny and did not thrive. Later, another baby's arm was burnt very badly when an older child knocked over a pot of boiling coffee, and again we were a part of their lives for a few days.

Simón began introducing his relatives and friends to us when they were in need of medical aid. He acted as intermediary, so we soon looked on him as our official interpreter for anyone who spoke the Zenzontepec Chatino language.

With all these varied visitors we are constantly reminded of the 'other Chatinos' beyond Tataltepec. The one time in the year when we see lots of them at once, is during the annual feast of the town's patron saint, the Ascension. This is the only occasion when there is a market held in the town square, and people flock in from all the surrounding towns and villages for this important fiesta. The local people take advantage of this market, and also of the visitors. They suddenly become very businesslike, and every family decides what they will sell at this time — usually something edible or drinkable. Some will have refreshment stands, manned by excited, but solemn and responsible, younger teenage daughters, with smaller sisters and brothers to run errands for them. They sell drinks made from wild lemons and tamarinds, and from locally grown watermelons, and also green coconuts. They sell fruit (mangoes grow wild, and are in season for Ascension Day), sweet bread rolls (with a generous amount of eggs in the mix, so that they melt in one's mouth), local coconut ice, and *tamales* (savoury pasties of shrimp, iguana, fish, pork, chicken, etc. — no need for a plate with the individual banana leaf wrappings). Some other little girls mingle with the crowd, carrying their wares in wide, shallow baskets on their heads.

The excitement begins the week before. It is an ordinary lovely sunny morning, with everyone quietly going about their routine work, when . . . bang, bang and BANG! People crowd out of the houses to see, and word ripples along from person to person, family to family: 'The firework-makers are arriving!' The chief firework-maker and his apprentices set up shop on the Town Hall verandah, and with a constant audience of small boys, start making fireworks — the more crackle and bang they have, the better. They are mostly decorated with crêpe paper in the national colours of red, white and green, except the animated models, which are made of papier mâché and stiff painted paper. There are black bulls with rockets on the horns, a catherine wheel on the tail, and earth-shaking bangers in the nostrils to finish up with. Some brave individual, who does not seem to mind being deafened, will get under this contraption on the great night of the fireworks display (the eve of Ascension Day), and prance around after the fuse is lit, to the delight of the crowd. He will drop to his knees as if the bull were dead, when those great bangers go off at the end. There are also dolls, both male and female, similarly wired up for the display. Then there are small set-pieces affixed to the Town Hall verandah pillars, and a most ingenious little 'plane' that rushes along a wire spitting fire, turns at the end, and tears back. The pièce de resistance is a '*castillo*'. A straight pole about forty feet long, is cut, trimmed, peeled and brought in from the mountainside by local lackeys. This is then wired up with rockets, bangers, catherine wheels, roman candles, and so on, to look like a tree again. The culminating triumph is a 'crown' at the top which shoots off at the end with a bang, after spinning round lit up. No wonder the firework-makers' arrival causes such excitement — the fiesta is beginning for sure now.

Hard on the heels of the firework-makers come the first traders, who set up their booths of clothing, jewellery, haberdashery, plastic bowls and buckets, little toys, etc. on the school verandah (the school's five classrooms are not all under one roof. The largest and oldest faces the town square, and boasts a very commodious verandah, like a colonnade, which seems to be considered common property) although the unfortunate teacher in charge of the class is expected to continue teaching. In succeeding days, a few more traders arrive, and the visitors begin to trickle in. Every visitor with a relative or some other — sometimes rather tenuous — link with a local family, turns up cheerfully at that house, confident of lodging for the duration of his stay. They will probably buy their food in the square.

This particular year, one enterprising local family put up a substantial shelter, with a tile roof, realistically remembering that the rainy season had begun. This became a restaurant, and another was set up in a shelter added to the end of a nearby house. This year also, another little awning appeared under a mango tree, with a table of literature underneath it — literature in both the national and local languages. Leslie had gone to the Town Hall and asked officially for permission for the stall. They told him the going rate, so he paid his rent and was given a receipt. When he returned with his awning and table, a councillor strolled over and suggested a good site for the stall. He seemed quite glad to see the books there.

On Ascension Day eve the fiesta began in earnest. Everybody selling in the square was doing a roaring trade, but one needed to watch those budding business-women at the refreshment tables!

The little stall with the books drew a steady stream of the curious, though not too many buyers. 'Ah, this is a dictionary in Spanish and Chatino!' Then, later — 'but it's the Chatino spoken here, not what my people speak. Don't you have any books for us?' 'Do you have any books in Mixteco? That can be written down too, you know!' 'No, we only speak Chatino, so we can only make books for the people here,' was our answer. 'Well, why don't you come and live in our town for a year to learn Santa Cruz Mixteco and make some books for us?' 'What about books for *us*?' said someone else. 'Yes, look — the pattern embroidered on your wife's blouse is here in this booklet,' I said. The mountain women immediately crowded forward to see. 'I embroider lots of blouse yokes, but I always copy from others — I've never had a paper,' said one. 'This paper speaks Chatino too. Listen.' 'That's just how we talk. Those pattern papers are *our* language.' Then, someone else who asked: 'What is this yellow book?' 'That's "The Old Words of God Himself" (the Old Testament Bible Stories). It's written in both Spanish and the Chatino of this area. This story of Noah, for instance, is on a record,' said Leslie. 'Oh, do you have records too?' 'Yes, indeed we do.'

Later we turned on the tape-recorder and played the local Chatino version of a Scripture passage from John's Gospel. A small crowd gathered immediately, and listened with wrapt attention, young and old alike. When the recorder stopped, they asked for more. 'Is that really what it says in that book? But I can't read.' 'Well, here's a very beginning reading book to start learning from, and here's another one that teaches all the Chatino letters and all the Spanish letters,' Leslie told them.

So the conversations went at the bookstall throughout the day, until, in the afternoon, a torrential downpour drove everyone under cover. The church, the school verandah, and the Town Hall verandah were suddenly crowded to capacity. In the lulls, the girls rushed out to their refreshment stands again, and clients popped up from all around. But night was coming on, and more rain threatened, so we packed the bookstall into its boxes, piled them into the wheelbarrow, and trundled it away to a nearby friend's house for the night.

At one point during the day some smiling, friendly men had come up to the bookstall, and introduced themselves as believers from Santa Cruz — so they must have been Mixtec people. Now we encountered three more believers, *mestizos* from El Paso this time. We had lodgers that night, and encouraging Christian fellowship. These believers had taken the opportunity of the fiesta to distribute pamphlets explaining salvation through faith in Jesus Christ, and encouraging Bible reading. They had visited a number of homes, and talked to people about Christ wherever they were invited in.

The fiesta certainly underlines the strategic location of Tataltepec! But when the celebrations are over and the visitors have dispersed to their homes, we often reflect on the situation of the 'other Chatinos' for whom there are no records or books. Sometimes we wonder if Simón is the key to these Zenzontepec Chatinos.

But meanwhile our main effort still lies with the Chatinos of Tataltepec. So far not many of them have responded but we have seen enough evidence of God's working in the lives of people like Reginalda, Florida and Terio to know that the translated Scriptures are a powerful and effective weapon in the hands of the Holy Spirit.

As we have seen Reginalda's testimony bear fruit in her son, so we look forward in faith to the day when many others will be able to say with her that they too have found 'the narrow trail leading to God's place'.

Epilogue

NEWS HAS RECENTLY arrived of another fiesta. This one was held in a different part of Mexico's southern mountains in a village that speaks a dialect of the Chinantec language. Just as among the Chatinos, where Leslie and Kitty Pride have been living, the fiesta was an occasion which made a colourful break from life's normal routine, something eagerly looked forward to and long remembered. But the occasion also had a special relevance to the Prides and to their purpose in living among the Chatinos.

The Chinanteco fiesta attracted an exceptional number of visitors to the little village where it was held. Every house was filled to capacity and many people had to sleep out in the surrounding coffee groves. The local villagers made the most of their refreshment-stall opportunities as strangers arrived a day or two before the start of the festival. Tortillas were brought in from all over the region in such quantities that the large bed-like structure where they were stored collapsed under the load and had to be shored up. 2,000 extra mouths take a lot of feeding!

A day or two before the fiesta started a number of boxes were brought in from the city by a Missionary Aviation Fellowship plane. These boxes were left unopened as those leading the fiesta wanted everyone who had made the journey to share the first sight of their contents together. For in these boxes were copies of the newly printed Chinanteco New Testament, which were to be dedicated at the fiesta.

Long before sunrise on the day of dedication, believers went to the church to sing hymns. When the service began at eight a.m. crowds of people had gathered round the tables which were piled high with the books. For more than an hour they listened to reports of leaders from each of the thirty-four congregations in thirty towns, who spoke of God's working among them. Many told of the darkness of personal sin and of how they had not known God before the coming of His Word in their own language.

The distribution of the New Testaments was planned in an unusual manner. The Chinantec leaders, convinced that the 1,000 copies of the New Testament available at the time of dedication (half the edition) would not be adequate to meet the demand of those wanting to buy, decided to limit purchases to one book per household at first. In that way 700 books were distributed in one day, and the Word of God went into virtually every town of the entire Chinantec area.

It was a great day too for Calvin and Carolyn Rensch, both from Pennsylvania, who had come to live among these villagers more than eighteen years earlier. During these years they had known many days that were filled so full with demands for medical help and other physical needs, that they left almost no time for language study and translation. For them too progress had often seemed painfully slow and the response of the villagers disappointing, but on this Dedication Day they could only look up to God with praise for what He had done and for the way He had enabled them to persevere when the way was hard.

The completed New Testament is not always dedicated with such a large and enthusiastic celebration. In other cases the good seed has not yet brought forth a hundredfold and there are only a handful of believers to welcome the Word as it is made available. We know from the teaching of our Lord Himself that different soils yield crops of different kinds. But we also know that those who sow the good seed should do so in certain hope of a harvest. It is this hope that sustains the translator and enables him to keep working and praying during the years of waiting.

In the preceding chapters Kitty has focused attention not upon herself and the work of translation, but upon the people of her adoption and their need for something more than bread. It is in the translator's every day contacts with his people that their hunger for spiritual food is aroused. The translator's task is not just to master a new language and translate the Scriptures into it; he must be available for God to use him as a means of awakening spiritual hunger — the hunger that God will Himself meet through His translated Word. So let the Chatino people, to whom you have been introduced in these pages, teach you how to pray for Bible translators throughout the world. Wycliffe is currently at work in more than 600 languages in thirty countries, while many hundreds of further languages have not yet received any part of God's Word to bring them spiritual life and food. We thank God that His tidings of great joy are indeed intended for all people.

David Bendor-Samuel
Home Director, 1975.

Appendix

1973	Florida died of pneumonia.
1974	Taurino died of dysentery and a tumour pressing on the spinal cord.
1975	The Gospel of John and the Acts of the Apostles were printed as separate books.
Early 1975	Ed and Linda Wardle arrived in Nopala to tackle the mountain Chatino language spoken in the eastern part of the county, the area farthest away from Tataltepec. It is a tremendous encouragement to have another Wycliffe team in the Chatino area.

Pronouncing Names

Oaxaca	wah-HA-kah
Mitla	MEET-lah
Juquila	who-KEE-lah
Yaitepec	yigh-tay-PECK
Zenzontepec	sen-sonn-tay-PECK
Tataltepec	tah-tahl-tay-PECK
Tututepec	two-two-tay-PECK